T0354555

Living Out A Dream

Living Out A Dream

PRISCILLA E. BAULDRY

authorHOUSE

AuthorHouse™
1663 Liberty Drive
Bloomington, IN 47403
www.authorhouse.com
Phone: 833-262-8899

Published by AuthorHouse 05/01/2024

ISBN: 978-1-4772-1976-8 (sc)
ISBN: 978-1-4772-1975-1 (hc)
ISBN: 978-1-4772-1974-4 (e)

Library of Congress Control Number: 2012910542

Print information available on the last page.

This book is printed on acid-free paper.

ACKNOWLEDGMENTS

Readers:
Ralph Bauldry, Craig Bauldry Sr., Donna Bauldry, Julie Beltowski, Patricia Smith, Chuck Smith, Jeanine Piotrowski, Courtney Piotrowski, Linda Smith, Sharon Northup

Typist:
Diana Smith Turchick

Editors:
Patricia Smith, Chuck Smith, Craig Bauldry, Darlene O'Brien, Sharon Northup

A special thank you to **Chuck** who did a major editing job.

Word processor and computer assistance:
Patricia Gross, Joyce Golden, Craigen Bauldry Jr., Jaren Bauldry, Eric Mausolf, Paige Beltowski

CONTENTS

THE END

NAME PRONOUNCIATION

Zenna (Zze na)

Gbandi (Gah band ee)

Ajani (Ah jon ee)

Chikae (Chic kay)

Kaela (kay la)

Ari (air ee)

Aza (Azz ah)

Paci (Pack ee)

Iman (ee mon)

INTRODUCTION

Just off a busy freeway in a small town in Michigan, a thirteen-year-old boy named Appy Olsen will soon come into manhood. Oftentimes, before vacationers continue their journey further north on Interstate-75, tired drivers will exit the expressway for a night's sleep in nearby West Branch motels. However, much deeper in Appy's town, the streets are lined with large, old Victorian period homes and overgrown oaks with spectacular green leaf tops. Most all the residents find the area's landscape to be morainic and beautiful. Moreover, crossing the railroad tracks and down the main street toward the far end of town is a brick and gated enclosure that leads to a large church, adjacent school, and an orphanage. These buildings are nestled on an acre or two of church land. Further in the town are many more acres of land where West Branch farmers supply St Matthew and the town folks with wholesome food.

Appy's mother abandoned him at birth. The orphanage was the only life he knew. Although he had many friends who came and went, and children of all ages who coexisted with him at the home, loneliness certainly persisted throughout his childhood. In addition, the older teens teased the younger boys relentlessly giving them two options…toughen up or run fast. Appy could run fast that's for sure. Fortunate for him, he had a favorite nun, Sister Jenny, who comforted him through his trials, but at times, she found him boyish enough to wear even her down.

Still, whenever he did something wrong as a young child Sister Jenny would kiss him on the forehead and say, "Appy, you'll do better tomorrow."

Appy would always look up at her with big sad eyes and reply, "Yes, Sister Jenny, I want to do better tomorrow."

In his younger years, he wasn't quite sure just what constituted a mischievous act, but he thought Sister Jenny to be very pretty. He also could feel her love for him.

Father Jeff, who headed St. Matthew, often related stories to Appy about the happenings in his childhood. Like the time he found a snake outside on the playground at school, put it in his pocket, and once inside the classroom began to whirl it atop his head hissing and yelling, 'Watch out this rattle snake has a hold on my thumb!'

"Appy, the story went that you stomped your feet. Started giggling wildly as the whole class and Sister Angie went screaming down the corridor and out the entrance door. Of course, you were marched down to my office by Father Larry who patrolled the school halls for any disturbances."

"Father Larry told me that you moped all the way down the hall trying to plead your case. Repeatedly you argued, 'What's so scary? It's only a garden snake.' When you entered my office Appy, you still had the snake in your pocket. Apparently, you wanted to keep it as a pet and expressed your wishes. 'It's small and cute. I want to keep it.' I had to remind you that I could see the snake had its head poking out and hissing. I then said, 'For heaven's sake Appy, put that snake out in the yard.' After you released the snake, I pointed my finger at you and declared, 'One more time my fine fellow, you'll find yourself in deep trouble.'"

Father Jeff loved to tell Appy these stories, "As punishment you had to make up beds in the girls' dorm three mornings in a row. Sister Angie could hear you mumbling, 'Sissy girls. Who needs em?' She also stood by the door with her hands on her hips seeming to enjoy seeing you punished. You can understand that now, I am sure. I related to you that the punishment was because I didn't appreciate all the little girls clinging on my arms crying and shaking—looking to me to console them and keep them safe. Because there were so many little girls, that was an awesome situation that you put me in. Of course, at that time, I needed to make a few things clear to you, Appy. Insisting that you keep your bed neat, your dorm orderly, which you were remiss about, and to keep snakes outside where they belong. After that, you never brought any more reptiles into the classroom.

Not-to-say there wasn't other irritating events where you needed to be gently disciplined."

Appy liked reminiscing with Father Jeff, as well. "I remember asking you what happened to the hair on top of your head. You chuckled saying, 'Someday you'll understand.' However, in my younger years, I related things to my own experiences. I was certain that Sister Angie and the girls probably lost a few hairs the way they acted over snake events. I thought that maybe a poisonous snake scared the hair clean off your head." Father Jeff found Appy's memory of events interesting since he was probably only six years of age at the time. Also extremely comical since his hair thinned when he was young. Moreover, he had made peace with that awhile back.

Appy enjoyed the evenings in the residence. He thought they were the very best. First, everyone would complete his/her homework. Then everybody enjoyed movies. The younger children watched their animated cartoons. The older children watched something more compatible to their age. Sister Eunice was in charge of entertainment. She was very good at planning events being open to new ideas. She'd separate the children in the gathering room according to age and preferences and let each age group choose an activity of interest to them. The little ones stayed up until 8:00 p.m., often falling asleep while watching such movies as "Bernie the Alligator." The older boys carried them off to their beds, inevitably, upsetting the girls by placing their movie on pause. The older children usually stayed up until 10:00 p.m. At that hour, they were usually tired out giving no resistance to the nuns. Being somewhat sheltered, Appy felt he learned much about the outside world from the movies he watched.

He enjoyed the winter months in West Branch often building snow borders on the lawn, lined it with plastic, filled it with water, and waited for it to freeze. When the ice was just right, he played hockey with the younger boys. Something he enjoyed a great deal. In addition, the children had picnics and games of baseball in the summer where even the girls played.

The Sisters often took the children to the zoo. The older girls and boys helped watch the younger ones. Even though Appy was a teen, he still enjoyed the zoo animals—especially the elephants. He was good about helping the Sisters with the young ones since he enjoyed their innocence.

When Appy turned fourteen, his voice began to crack. Even Father Jeff would tease him about the left out portions of his sentences. Quite appropriately, at this age, the Fathers gave the boys a book on puberty, a movie on the subject, and a question and answer session where nobody raised any questions for fear of asking something stupid. Appy certainly was becoming tall and handsome, but his mind was troubled after watching many friends acquire parents and siblings. Almost every weekend couples would walk through the gathering room, sit next to a child, and whisper sweetly to them. Several weeks later that child was mysteriously gone.

Appy often thought, *"What's wrong with me?"*

He knew he could take the garbage out—that must be worth something. He also knew that he no longer was disrespectful to Father Jeff or the nuns at the schoolhouse. It began to become quite clear to Appy's senses that people seemingly wanted very young children—not grown teenage boys. Missing his chance of having adoptive parents he realized he could hope all his life for something that might never happen. Only once in the past did a couple sit down next to him. The pounding of his heart went on for weeks as he dreamed good dreams, but much to his heart's calling nothing came of it. The St. Matthew staff was beginning to see that Appy was becoming a very good teen. When he was taking driver's training, Father Larry told him, "Appy, you and I will drive around the school parking lot on the weekends for practice."

"That's super!" He answered.

Sister Jenny appointed herself to take him for his first driver's test, even though; he had no job or car.

Appy passed his test saying to Father Larry, "I'm thrilled about getting my driver's license and grateful to you and Sister Jenny for all your help in preparing me."

"Well Appy," Father Larry answered, "We're here to help you—not to hinder you in anyway."

Lately, Father Jeff was putting a great deal of trust in him, as well. Appy was past the stage of disappointing him anymore. Appy felt that Sister Jenny and Father Jeff must be what parents are all about—not knowing exactly what real parents were like.

As other children entered and left St Matthew, and Appy was well into his teens, he entrenched himself in reading and computers. He no longer went to the gathering room on the weekends.

Appy always seemed to have sincere feelings for the little ones at St. Matthew. He often asked the Sisters, "Do you mind if I hold and feed the baby?"

He spent time cooing to them—helping the Sisters out. Although most of the time he worked very hard on his studies. Sister Jenny knew that Appy would be graduating from high school in a couple of years. She insisted he attend college. It was time to search out colleges for him because she knew Appy could pull down scholarships and grants. She thought he could take two years for an associate degree at Kirtland Community College, and then attend Saginaw Valley State University for his bachelor degree. He could drive Sister's car to a parking area along Interstate-75 where he could join with other students to share the commute and gas expenses.

Soon after Appy graduated from high school, he enrolled and attended college at Kirtland CC, always doing superbly in his college environment. He definitely needed a place to stay. Father Jeff and Sister Jenny were happy to continue to provide him with room and board throughout his four-year stretch at college. Father Jeff paid him to wash cars and windows—many windows. Appy also chauffeured Father Jeff and the Sisters around town.

Father Jeff was quite the conversationalist. Everywhere the two went together, when leaving, he'd bless the people with the sign of the cross saying, "Never forget the children." The town was always very generous with St. Matthew. Both carpenters and plumbers would show up to help the church out. Appy also continued to help the Sisters. Every week he drove them to the farms for eggs, veggies, and apples; helped Father Jeff with his computer problems often; and did the bookkeeping and accounting chores that Father Jeff seemed to detest so.

Father Jeff often told Appy, "I'm not sure what I'd do without your help."

Appy was not certain whether Father Jeff sincerely meant that, or if he was trying to make him feel good. Either way, he sucked that up like a sponge. He rather enjoyed comments like that, especially coming from Father Jeff who seemed to be his hero.

"Oh thanks, Father Jeff."

The contributors of St. Matthew agreed to keep Appy at the home because he was diligently applying himself toward a successful future. Many of the other boys left St. Matthew's home without permission before eighteen, but Appy made no attempt at that. He often wondered what became of them. The Board of Directors thought that Appy would make a good poster child helping St. Matthew's reputation immensely. Selfish as that might seem, it kept Appy where he needed to be.

After four years of college, Appy graduated on the Dean's list with a Bachelor Degree in Electrical Engineering, but his computer skills went far beyond his college experience. He could without much strain rebuild and repair them. He had an itch for designing them, as well. Of course, internet knowledge was also high on his list of priorities. His talent amazed St. Matthew's staff. Everyone admired him when the computers crashed; and Appy would say, "No problem—they're easy to fix."

It happened so frequent to St. Matthew's computers that needless-to-say Appy's ability in electronics made him a very valuable resident. For sure, one who contributed to reducing cost for repairs. Father Jeff was always bragging about Appy's talent letting everyone know how lucky St. Matthew was to have him. With his degree in hand, Appy knew he had to start looking for a career opportunity in the outside world. He'd have to think once again about his future outside the home. It definitely was going to be a tough and lonely process that he was sure would cause him a bit of stress. It was unavoidable. He knew that for sure.

One evening at the dinner table, Father Jeff asked Appy if he'd join Sister Jenny and him in his office when their meal was finished.

Appy wondered to himself, *"What's up?"*

At the meeting, Father Jeff began to tell Appy that he was leaving St. Matthew for a mission in Nairi, Africa.

Appy's heart began to pound. His eyes widened quite remarkably. He solemnly spoke, "Oh Father, what'll the children do without you?"

"Its okay, Appy," Father Jeff could visually detect how shocked Appy looked. "Father Larry is more than capable of caring for the duties here at St. Matthew and Sister Jenny will assist him."

"Oh yes Appy, I'll be here to see that the children are washed, dressed, eat their meals on time, and attend school."

Appy shouted, "I know how capable you are, Sister!"

Sister Jenny was puzzled at the alarming tone in his voice.

"Oh, Sister Jenny, I'm sorry. It just dawned on me that the foundation I've always relied on is about to crumble. I feel I haven't had time to figure out my next step after having graduated."

Father Jeff sensing Appy's feelings, "Never be afraid, Appy. I'm sure you'll do just fine once you leave us. It's just another step forward in growing up. You've made many steps already on your own."

"I hope you're right Father because I am feeling upset right now."

Appy took Father Jeff's leaving as a means of abandoning him when he wasn't ready for that kind of break. He pounced on Sister Jenny thinking she didn't stop this from happening. After all, she was his protector throughout his life.

"Appy, this might make you feel better," Father Jeff said. "I've asked you to join us here this evening to find out if you might like to go to Nairi with me. I think it might be a very good experience for you before you begin a new career of your own."

Appy had felt his heart pound like that before. "I might love that, Father Jeff."

Appy shook Father Jeff's hand. At twenty-three he had no idea where he'd find work, or for that matter, what path he'd take to support himself. He reached across Father Jeff and kissed Sister Jenny on the forehead.

"Oh gosh," he said, "I've internalized your behavior, Sister Jenny."

She smiled slightly. Her cheeks turned a perfect shade of pink.

That night in bed Appy thought about what Nairi would be like, "*No need to worry,*" he said to himself, "*Father Jeff, will be there.*" He felt so relieved that Father Jeff wasn't leaving him behind.

CHAPTER 1

On the airplane to Nairi, Father Jeff was making small talk with Appy—something he enjoyed doing.

"How many children do you want, Appy?"

"Oh, I've been thinking anywhere between twelve to twenty-four."

"Wee, that's a lot of children for one couple!" With a twist of his head and a slight smile, "You might change your mind about that once you marry and settle down. Without a doubt, your wife may have some reservations about that many children."

"Do you think so, Father? I've given much thought about this. Maybe I'll have twelve, but I'll leave myself open for more."

Ever since Appy was a small boy, Father Jeff found that Appy tickled his senses. After the snake episode, he found himself chuckling aloud in his sleep. He was sure even the Sisters laughed once they got over the excitement of the day. Oftentimes in meetings, the group spoke of some of the antics children pulled and found they were very amused.

The casual conversation continued and Father Jeff explained to Appy.

"We'll be bringing six to twelve children back to the home at St. Matthew. Some of the children in Nairi are orphans due to AIDS. This disease is directly responsible for the death sentence passed upon their parents. These conditions prompted Nairi's health committee to come up with a plan that would jump start world leaders to promote the needs of these children by placing them in orphan homes for global adoption. Most are infants, some two and three-year-olds. There are older children, as well. I believe we'll be in Nairi at least two years choosing children who we're sure aren't ill—also children who'll be capable of adjusting in a completely new environment. Most of the children have learned English from the Sisters and workers at Sisters of Amity where they live. The Sisters of Amity orphanage has housed these orphans, but they're extremely overburdened, lacking in space and qualified people in areas of schooling and medicine. Without outside assistance, the future of these children could be dismal at best. The contributors feel that the children need one on one attention that'll be meaningful in building character and sociality. It definitely needs to be addressed."

"Did you know Appy that many countries, states, and providences around the world will provide these orphan homes with support for these disadvantaged children much like Family Care recipients receive? The burden won't be left up to contributors who might not want to be world protectors."

Appy seemed enthralled at the grown-up response from leaders. "Father, even at my age and with my education, I have a great deal to learn."

Appy also felt a pain in his heart for all the babies and toddlers. At this moment though, he knew he wanted to delay this painful conversation.

"That was interesting Father, but do you mind if I change the subject some?"

"No, not at all—what's on your mind, Appy?"

Appy continued, "Well then, I spent time on the internet before coming on the plane and clicked on Nairi's animals. Did you know that they have five big animals' lions, rhinos, buffalos, leopards, and elephants within Nairi's borders? I'm not sure you know this Father Jeff, but Sister Jenny knows that I love elephants. I just want you to know should you be asked out on a Safari, I'm game."

"Appy, I hope we can have some fun, but I think both you and I are going to be very busy."

When landing at Nairi's airport, a man came forward and introduced himself to Appy and Father Jeff. While shaking hands with both men, he said his name was Rahl. Rahl began to ask Father Jeff if he was tired from the flight—moreover, if he wanted to go straight to the mission house to put away his belongings and have some dinner?

"Rahl, that sounds good. By the way, my name is, Father Jeff. This young fellow is, Appy."

"Appy—that's different, I've never heard that name before. It's good to meet you both. This is a good cause. I applaud the response the States and St. Matthew have made. It'll make a difference to these poverty stricken Nairian children."

That evening at supper Rahl whispered to Appy, "You'll be shocked when you witness the children at the village community and their surroundings for the first time."

"Really, what'll shock me the most in your estimation?"

"Well, if I had to choose," Rahl answered. "I'd say the sadness in the children's eyes. I often wonder be this fear I'm seeing, or a lack of affection, or simple idleness without proper play; on the other hand, maybe its poor nutrition, confusion, sickness, and the deaths of family members. It'd take a damn good psychologist to come up with the thoughts and feelings of these children. I'm sure having a difficult time figuring it out with my line of studies."

Appy's stomach began to do flip-flops. *"Bon* appetit*"* just wasn't happening as he tried to envision what Rahl was saying. He wondered if he could emotionally handle those precious and strickened eyes. One thing for sure Appy sensed Rahl to be a sensitive, gentle male. What he wasn't aware of was that Rahl would become a best friend for life.

That night in his sleep, he dreamt of small eyes that were flashing dark accusations and saying,

"If you can't stand looking at our eyes, you're the enemy. Go home, you'll be of no help here."

Appy woke suddenly, got out of bed sweating, half-asleep. He went to the kitchen for a glass of milk. He thought he'd rather have something stronger that might knock him out this night. He hated dreams like this.

Early morning came. Father Jeff woke, Appy.

"Appy—Rahl wants to take us to meet Father Reed and the children out at Sisters of Amity. He'd like to get an early start. I'll hustle up some grub for the three of us. You can busy yourself dressing."

Appy yawned. He really felt he needed more sleep, but he mumbled in an alto voice, "Okay, Father."

In the meantime, Rahl pulled his dirt-rich jeep up in front of the mission house. He readied himself for the ride putting on a gray khaki jacket and a four-cornered hat with netting hanging from it.

At the breakfast table, Appy asked Rahl, "How far is it to Sisters of Amity?"

"Sisters of Amity is about ten dusty miles and a trillion flies away, Ap."

Appy chuckled, "You have a way with words, Rahl."

Appy looked at Father Jeff and asked, "Did you think to bring any bug juice?"

Father Jeff winked, "We're all set on that score since I'm one step ahead of those little black, winged devils who somehow think I'm cotton candy. I wouldn't be without it."

"Okay, good. I never gave it a thought being more interested in bringing deodorant in this kind of heat."

Rahl put his hand on Appy's shoulder and declared, "Around here that's funny, Ap, since amenities like that mean nothing at all in these parts."

Appy jokingly said, "You mean I have to smell how ripe you guys get?" Appy had never experienced anyone calling him "Ap" before. After all, he lived a somewhat sheltered life, but he rather liked the shortened version of his name. As they climbed into the jeep, Appy asked, "Hey Rahl, where did you get that "one-of-a-kind hat?""

Rahl chuckled slightly, "My girl friend Ruthy made it—looks awful I know, but it keeps them damn flies from eating at my eyeballs. You'll want Ruthy to make a "one-of-a-kind" head cover like this for you. You'll meet Ruthy soon."

"That'll be wonderful." Appy answered. "What's your line of work here, Rahl?"

"I'm a journalist. I work for International Magazine. I'm working on a piece for the magazine on Nairi's orphaned children."

"Wow, you have my attention! Where did you attend college?"

"I attended two colleges—Saginaw Valley State University in Saginaw, and Northern Michigan University in Marquette—both in Michigan.

Appy replied with great excitement in his voice, "What a coincidence, Rahl. I'm from Michigan, too. Moreover, I went to Saginaw Valley State University. We may have passed each other in the halls while changing classes. I live in West Branch where do you live?"

"I live in Saginaw—maybe only sixty miles from you."

Appy stunned somewhat, "You're right, how strange."

Exchanging smiles, the two men fist bumped. Father Jeff was enjoying the fact that Appy and Rahl were getting along so well. It would make Appy's experience in this new country so much richer.

He thought to himself, "*Thank you, Lord.*"

"What was your specialty in college, Ap?"

"I have an Electrical Engineering Degree, majoring in computer electronics. I repair computers, too."

"Gee Ap; we have four computers at the mission house, not one works. None of us has cell phones here because we make the choice between that expense and a computer bill. Most of us would rather have the world news, facebook, games, and the like. I'd sure like to document my notes on my word processor."

"I'll take a look at them, Rahl, and try to get at least one up and running."

Father Jeff let Rahl know, "He's an expert."

"That's a deal, Ap. Coincidentally, my dad owns a large computer manufacturing plant. I could put in a good word for you. He's always looking for bright staff to head departments. He especially needs someone to teach complicated repair skills to other associates."

Father Jeff enthusiastically piped in, "That could prove to be a good opportunity for you, Appy."

"Oh yes, but for now I need to keep my mouth shut. I am eating dust. My throat's getting dry."

Father Jeff handed him a piece of the candy he brought for the children.

"Thanks Father. That'll help. My throat is really irritated."

The talk had calmed down somewhat. Rahl spotted a dog in the distance.

"Oh, here comes, Ladi."

He pulled over and loaded Ladi between Father Jeff and Appy.

"Ladi is kind of a mascot around these parts. She has seemingly adopted me as her master. She'll sit perfectly still, stares straight ahead, until she can be with the children. Of course, the toddlers are good at feeding small bits of their food to her. There's a bag of dog food back there. We should stop just before we get to the home to feed her, so she isn't such a pest around the children. She usually stays at the mission house at night. I'm not sure what she's doing five miles out like this!"

"We're getting close," Rahl, said, "We should stop to feed Ladi." When outside the jeep, the men brushed the caked dust from their clothes.

"Gosh—Rahl," Appy asked, "Did you have to get use to this climate? The heat and biting dust, I mean. This dust stings my face."

"Oh yes," Rahl answered.

He put Ladi's bowl of food down. The three watched as Ladi gobbled it down as if she'd never get anymore.

Father Jeff asked Rahl, "What kind of dog is, Ladi?"

"She's a mix I believe between collie and shepherd. She's kind of a cute mongrel, smart and protective of the children. I've grown close to her, but I'm not sure I'll bring her home when I leave. I want to ask Ruthy to marry me. Unfortunately, she has allergies to long hair animals. She takes pills that allow her to be near, Ladi. It's a lot to ask of her to put up with me and my dog."

Appy inquired, "Why's Ruthy here in Nairi, Rahl?"

"She works for Humanity Search. When she gets back home, she'll gather churches and charity organizations to meet the overwhelming needs of the Nairian people. The needs here will include everything from dresses, tee shirts, long pants for boys and men, shorts, diapers, bottled water, to formula for babies whose mothers have AIDS."

Father Jeff commented, "She does good work, Rahl. I applaud her. I'll enjoy talking with her soon."

While standing along side the jeep, waiting for Ladi to do her business, Appy was taking in the scenery. He commented on the landscape.

"The trees look so top heavy and lacy. Trees that monkeys could enjoy, but offer no privacy or shade that humankind can appreciate. I must say, I do like the billowing clouds that seemingly hang low enough to kiss one's cheek then scoot away across the sky. I read somewhere that the mountains off in the distance come from cracks in the earth where lava seeped through and formed them."

"Yes," Rahl declared. "That's a good liking of Nairi. Soon, you'll be adding flies to that description."

"Is that a community in the distance, Rahl?" Father asked.

"That's the poorest of the poor. That's the village people I told you about, Ap."

"Can we stop there?" Father Jeff asked.

"Maybe coming back would be a good time, if it isn't too late. Father Reed is expecting to feed us some lunch. The cooks at Sisters of Amity are very good. You'll not want to miss this feast."

"Later, will work just fine," Appy, chuckled.

Rahl gave Ladi a command, "Okay, Ladi girl, get in the jeep. We're on our way again."

As they pulled into the grounds at Sisters of Amity, Father Reed was waiting at the door entrance. The priests and nuns living quarters looked square shaped with flat roofs and dusty brick walls. If the bricks were a color once, they changed overtime. The housing quarters for the children looked much the same.

Father Reed came close to the jeep with a big smile, "You must be Father Jeff and Appy. It's so good to meet you." Father Jeff and Appy shook hands with Father Reed. Father Reed cheerfully invited all three to, "Come in and we'll have some lunch and talk."

Father Jeff reciprocated, "It's also good to meet you, Father Reed. Rahl has said many good things about your presence in Nairi. I hope I can earn some admiration while I'm here."

Father Reed answered, "It doesn't take much effort. The peoples' lives are very simple here."

The men carried on for an hour or so talking about everything from their flight, their night at the mission, and even Ladi who was waiting patiently to see the children as she sat very close to the door.

Father Reed said, "That's one fine dog! Well, what do you say if we walk over to see the children now before Ladi takes off on her own?"

Father Jeff replied, "Of course, we'd like that—lead the way."

Appy decided to stay a little in the background. Let Father Jeff do what he did best, "polite conversation."

When entering the children's living space, one could hear chattering and somewhat busy background noise.

"Forgive the noise, schools out today. The children are enjoying themselves," said a Sister as she passed by the three.

Baby cribs were leaned against the four walls that housed the infants, and in the center of the big room, sitting pads for those tots who no longer needed cribs. Appy went near the cribs. He waited until a baby raised her arms.

"Do you want to be picked up, sweetness? You're so cute in your little girl dress." He began to baby talk to the infant and tickled her neck. Appy was seldom without a baby in his arms.

Father Reed remarked, "We're so crowded here. I feel these children should have parents for special attention; whereas here, the time is spent feeding, diapering, dressing, teaching, preparing meals, and bedtime readiness which doesn't leave much time for holding them, sports, or having fun with them."

"Well," Father Jeff proclaimed, "We're here to take anywhere from six to twelve children home with us. We'd like them to be highly adoptable, healthy young children. It'd make no sense to bring the children from one country to another or from one orphan home to another without a high probability of adoption."

"Of course," Father Reed answered.

Off to the side, Father Jeff began to tell Father Reed about, Appy. "Appy was one of the orphans who had never been adopted. I met his mother. She had him out of wedlock. She definitely was a middle class girl who seemed to exhibit a basic genetic goodness. I'm sure she thought someone would adopt him; and he'd be happy with his new parents. He was a most desirable Caucasian boy. We gave him the name Appy because we were all convinced that he was "Apt" to be successful in life. It broke my heart that he was unable to have a family. You might say that one of the Sisters at St. Matthew and I took him under wing and guided him this far. We care about him, deeply."

"Father Jeff, what an experience this is for him to come to Nairi!"

"Oh yes, simply wonderful. Appy is very innovative. When he was about twelve, we gave him our old computers since he was so interested in them. He became a superb repairperson for us. I think he liked using computers for homework and games. It inspired him."

"Well, you have sold me on, Appy. I've some wireless computers here in bad need of repair. I know nothing about computers. When they are working, I am lucky to get the news in the morning. I can pay him a little to help him with spending money for his stay here."

"Oh, that'd be so kind of you. I'll tell Appy on our way back to the mission. I know Rahl will be good enough to transport him here."

"Well, I'm going to try to accommodate you and Appy here, so that you can be around the children and eat well."

"Swell, if I never have to suffer the dusty drive out here in Rahl's jeep again, you can bet that would please me as well as, Appy."

Appy, with baby in arms, stopped to talk to some of the Sisters. They filled him in on the devastation that rape and AIDS have brought upon these children.

Sister Myra mentioned, "You're the first of the homes to come to their rescue, so you'll be remembered. Rahl says that we'll all be in his magazine piece on Nairi."

"Oh, I never gave that a thought, but I suppose you're right. Sister Myra, do the children play baseball?"

"No, but they play a game of sorts that they made up with sticks and stones resembling hockey or cricket."

"I'd like to teach the boys and girls the game of baseball. I've some equipment with me. I'll also write the Sisters at St. Matthew for more through donations."

"No problem with learning the game of baseball. The children will enjoy anything that's not boring; I love baseball, so maybe I could be the coach's assistant coach." Sister Myra said—looking for approval.

"You're hired! You'll certainly make a great assistant coach."

Appy handed the little girl to Sister Myra for a diaper change. He headed back to the cribs to pick up another crying little person.

Appy said sweetly in a quiet voice, "What's the matter little one? Let me help dry those tears."

Appy bottle-fed the baby in one of two rockers that Sisters of Amity had. The baby fell asleep in his arms. The child looked very peaceful with his head slightly hanging. He was out for sure.

Father Jeff walked by. He quietly asked, "What do you have there, Appy, one of the twelve?"

"I wish," was Appy's reply.

"I've some good news for you, Appy. I'll tell you all about it on the way home."

"Oh good Father; I especially enjoy good news." Appy answered.

Appy put the sleeping baby in the crib. Moreover, he was now trying to warm up to the toddlers who were sitting on their mats. He pulled out some very soft chocolate candy spooning small portions to the children. He cleaned the spoon each time with a wipe that Sister Myra gave him. As Appy sat on his own mat, he became popular quickly and many toddlers were standing above him.

"My name is, Appy. What are your names?"

Two answered, "I Zenna," "I Jimi."

Appy thought to himself, *"How cute is that!"*

Much time had passed. Rahl pulled his jeep up to the main door, walked in the home to inform Appy and Father Jeff that the time had come to head back to the mission. Ladi kissed the toddlers' good-bye, liking the sugar on their lips. Anyway, she was happy to see, Rahl. She followed him out to the jeep. Ladi usually gave him a harder time when it was time to leave.

Before they left, Father Reed told Father Jeff, "The two rooms that are open belong to two Sisters who went deeper in the bush to assist children. The Sisters here will clean and ready the rooms for you and Appy. It'll take a couple of days to clear everything out, but I'll let you know when we're ready."

Appy came out with a computer to take to the mission with him, telling Father Reed, "I'm going to try to repair one computer for the mission house, and one for Sisters of Amity—that way we can all communicate with each other."

Father Reed said, "That'll be wonderful, how about that, Rahl?

"Give that man a cigar!" Rahl waived his crossed fingers in the air.

It came natural for Father Jeff to say, "No need to cross your fingers Rahl—say a prayer. Our Lord is in need of prayers."

"You're right," answered Rahl.

Rahl wasn't much on religion, but he understood what Father Jeff was saying. He felt if anyone was perfect for the priesthood, Father Jeff fit the bill.

It was quiet going back. Everyone was feeling a little tired. One would guess that when you're with many noisy babies and toddlers a little quiet wasn't a bad thing.

As they got close to the village community, Rahl asked, "Do you two feel up to this today? How about we get close, but not stay long?"

The men nodded, "Yes."

When pulling up, Appy gasped, "These—are the eyes Rahl spoke of."

The children's eyes bulged out due to a lack of fat around them and their stomachs protruded noticeably. The scene caused sadness in Appy. As he turned his back, tears welled. Rahl put his hand on Appy's shoulder.

"Oh Rahl, how can this be?"

"I've no idea, Ap. However, I've learned that I can't correct all the problems and conditions in the world. I can report them hoping people like you and Father Jeff offer some help."

"SOME?" Appy said with a raised voice. "SOME?" He said again. "What an indictment on mankind!"

Appy's dream began to surface. He heard again, "*If you can't look into our eyes, you're not needed here, go home.*"

Appy turned around swiftly. He saw Father Jeff walking meaninglessly beside the jeep with his fist pressed against his lips. Appy went to Father Jeff and embraced him.

Father Jeff whispered, "Are you all right, Appy?"

Appy simply answered, "It's our turn to do our best. It'll not be easy for either of us."

Father Jeff patted him on the back, "Appy that's an intelligent and reasonable response to this situation. You make me proud!"

While once again brushing off the dust from their clothes, a black-skinned male approached the barbed wire fence.

"P*arlez vous francias*," he said

"O*ui*," Appy answered, "J*e m' appelle,* Appy."

"J*e m' appelle,* Brent."

"Father Jeff—Rahl, this man's name is, Brent."

The two men, surprised that Appy even spoke French, nodded their heads in Brent's direction.

"Father Jeff—I can see Ap is going to be an enormous asset to us here in Nairi."

Brent explained to Appy, "This is a very poor community. Many of our children leave here to go to Sisters of Amity because their parents are too sick to care for them or have died. Many people in Africa who have AIDS live very short lives; maybe only reach thirty-four years of age. The doctors from town come and volunteer their time to watch for immediate health issues." Brent took them to his living site that looked much like camping out to Appy.

Brent's wife said, "*Je suis,* Kaela."

"B*onjour,* Kaela," Appy said.

After a threesome conversation between Appy, Brent, and Kaela, Rahl broke in,

"Appy, do you see that gash on their son's leg?"

"Yes,—Brent told me, he caught it on that barbed wire fence out there where the jeep sits."

"Gee Ap, tell Brent that the boy's leg needs cleaning out and stitches before infection sets in. Wounds like that need special attention here in Nairi. Tell him we'll be back to pick him and his son up tomorrow to bring them to the hospital. By the way Ap, we need to go, we're not equipped with rubber gloves or long sleeve shirts. I usually carry them in the jeep, but I wasn't planning on coming this way today."

"Yes—Appy we should go," replied Father Jeff—not wanting to put Appy in any danger or Rahl or himself for that matter.

"Okay guys give me a chance here." Appy turned to explain to Brent as best he could since his French wasn't perfect. "Brent, we have to leave for today to return to the mission house before dark, but we'll be back sometime tomorrow to pick up you and your son."

There didn't seem a need to tell Brent a time because Appy was sure that he had no clock.

Everyone was somewhat quiet on the rest of the journey home until Ladi began barking nonstop. Rahl stopped the jeep thinking she had to relieve herself. Ladi jumped out. She ran from the jeep.

Rahl stunned by her reaction, "What the hell is with her? I guess I'll have to follow her." Ladi headed forward to a dug out shelter under a tree.

"Oh look," Appy, said, "two little puppies."

"They're Ladi's pups," Father Jeff added. "They have her markings."

Rahl still somewhat in shock said, "Gee, we need to load them up. I guess I've become a grandpa of sorts."

Ladi's pups moaned all through the nursing process. After all, it was a very long day without mom.

Rahl thinking aloud said, "Now it makes perfect sense why she was out here, but I wish she had come home to the mission house. I'd have given her a comfortable blanket to birth them on—poor thing."

After what the three had just witnessed, these baby pups were a bit of joy.

"So cute," Father Jeff commented. "Do you think, Rahl, there's a wolf out here? There doesn't seem to be any other dogs around here."

"Oh, there's a wolf all right."

Everyone laughed at Rahl's remark. Back at the mission house, Appy continued to work on computers. He didn't feel much like talking. Father Jeff and Rahl were resting quiet, as well. After all, the day had been long and the village community disturbing.

CHAPTER 2

In the morning, Father Jeff and Rahl went for a morning walk. Appy stayed at the mission house with Ladi and her pups. He had repaired one of the computers last night. Rather than work on another today, he thought he'd write, Sister Jenny.

> Dear Sister Jenny,
>
> Father Jeff and I are adjusting to the climate and have met the head priest at Sisters of Amity, Father Reed. He's a very nice priest, polite in mannerisms. Father Jeff and I like him. We also met a man named Rahl who's a journalist. He stays at the mission. He's doing a piece on the orphans in Nairi. He also drives us in his jeep to Sisters of Amity and back. He took us to a very poor camp on the plains. The flies were horrific there. The site seemed to have many sanitation problems. The children's eyes are bulged with enlarged stomachs due to poor nutrition—its one thing to view this scene in a magazine and quite another to witness

this in person. Father Jeff and I leaned on each other for support and comfort. Coming into the village, one could see stretches of mud-like home sites with shiny tin roofs that seemed held up with dirt blocks as beams for support. Some huts had Nairi soil on top of the tin where vegetation grew on its own. We met a man named Brent and his wife Kaela there. These people speak French only and seemingly enjoyed conversing with me. He took us to his home that looked more like a campsite, and introduced us to his family. His son who's twelve had a nasty gash in his leg. Rahl and I are bringing him to the hospital today to get it cleaned out and stitched. The boy's parents seemed very pleased. I'm glad that you convinced me to take three years of French in high school. I'm able to pick up half of what Brent says, but he senses that and throws out one word sentences until I eventually catch on. I have always been better at writing and reading French than speaking it.

Sister Jenny, I've an enormous favor to ask of you. The boys and girls have no activities at Sisters of Amity. I find that a shame. The children need to interact with each other and with the adults around them. I want to teach them baseball. I need equipment like mitts, baseballs, and wood bats for all ages. Could you ask Father Larry to announce at Mass that the people of Africa are looking for donations of used baseball equipment? We don't need new ones to make the game fun. I also need a baseball cap for Sister Myra who has been gracious enough to volunteer her help by being my assistant coach. The children would love hats, too, but I don't want to put you under any more pressure than wanted.

I'll soon make some money repairing computers. I'll send it to help pay for air postage fees. Let me know the cost involved. I need to do this for these precious five, six, seven, eight, nine, ten, and eleven-year-olds. All boys and girls twelve years and up will help in the games as cheerleaders, umps, instructors, and one scorekeeper. I want all to participate. I believe that'll be very important to these children. I miss you and everybody there. Say, hello, to Father Larry and let him know that I'll write him soon."

Appy

The men came back from their walk. Appy asked Rahl, "What time are we going to the camp to pick up Brent and his son? By the way, Rahl, did you catch what their son's name is?"

"No damn, I never asked. I was thinking around one o'clock, Ap. How would that suit you?"

"That's okay; I'll just continue to work on Father Reed's wireless. If I get it up and running, maybe we can drop it off at Sisters of Amity."

"Father Reed would like that, Ap."

Appy raised his brow, "It looks like it needs a battery. I hope that I can find one that still has juice in the parts that Father Reed gave me. I need to order some parts for him eventually, but they're not cheap. A battery could cost around a hundred bucks. I wonder if the mission contributors will allow an expense for something like that."

"Oh, I'm not sure, Ap, but money is somewhat scarce around here."

"Yeah, you might be right." Appy answered.

Father Jeff broke in, "I'll put together some tuna sandwiches, potato chips with a fruit dish for lunch."

"Yum," Appy said.

Rahl indicated that that would be fine. "After lunch, Ap, we'll leave for the camp."

Father Jeff insisted, "I'm going to stay here at the mission house to baby-sit Ladi and her pups, so she doesn't take a notion to bring them back to where they were born. We should name these pups soon."

Rahl shot back, "Tonight while sitting around we'll throw out names and see what fits these little dears. Let me see, what do we have here? Oh, the little one is a gal. The bigger one is a guy. This time I should have them neutered. I hope there's a vet in town that performs these surgeries. I have to assume there is. I know Ruthy isn't going to be overjoyed about my grandpa status." He chuckled.

"Well—grandpa, will you please set the table," Father Jeff requested. "I'll begin lunch?"

Appy continued to work on Father Reed's computer.

On a dusty, arid drive to Brent's village, Appy mentioned to Rahl that Brent said he was the leader of his village. He reports directly to the government in Nairi. If he finds someone doing a crime against another, he turns him/her into the police in the big town.

"Oh, no wonder he seemed so polite and friendly. I've been around him before and sensed his demeanor as that of someone educated."

"Yes, he went to college in France. His wife Kaela has a teaching degree. The two came here as missionaries hoping to stay for just a few years. Off to the side, he told me that his wife has HIV from a rape sustained while being here."

"Oh gee, Ap, that's so sad and disturbing!"

"Yes, her illness caused them to spend all they had. Brent took this job to get the free medicine and treatment. He said her outlook is good, but many in his village will die. He also said that not many people in Nairi want to care for or raise orphans and Sisters of Amity is their only other hope."

"Do you suppose, Ap, that they're afraid they might bring a disease into their homes—maybe just plain fearful of the disease?"

"I wouldn't doubt that, Rahl, with so much death all around them. I know every child is tested and examined for HIV before entering Sisters of Amity orphanage—to me that points to Brent as the protector of the living, sick, and dying in this French village."

"Wow, Ap, that's so sad, but nevertheless great that you're able to relate this to me for my magazine piece. Of course, I assure you I won't use real names. Let's make a pact, Ap, that we do something for Brent's family when we get back home."

"Yes, that'd definitely be a nice thing to do Rahl."

Rahl parked his jeep in the emergency parking area of the hospital. Lamar seemed a bit nervous.

Appy patted him on the back, "No worry, Lamar, the doctor will numb that sucker—you won't feel anything."

The emergency room staff called in a pediatrician to handle the large wound Lamar had. In the meantime, blood needed drawing for HIV testing—a routine lab check in Nairi.

A female doctor entered the room. She softly asked, "What's your name young man?" She stood apart from the hospital staff since she was Caucasian, spoke good English, and appeared to be American.

Appy answered, "Lamar is his name. He's a French speaking teen."

"Well Lamar, my name is, Dr. Sarah."

With protective gloves on, she looked at his wound. Appy thought, *"Dr. Sarah is absolutely beautiful.* He was finding it difficult to speak in her presence. Rahl took over. He wondered what was up with, Ap. He seemed to have a frog in his throat. Dr Sarah felt that she needed to put in about ten stitches.

"It's a large wound, so we'll need to keep him on antibiotics to protect him from infection."

Lamar now numbed was relaxing. Appy said in French, "You're brave, Lamar."

Rahl told Dr. Sarah, "We need to leave in short order. We're going to Sisters of Amity where Appy will be living soon to drop off a computer that he repaired for the clergy there. What's our next step with Lamar?"

"Well," Doctor Sarah answered. "He needs to take the antibiotics for ten days and return here to have the stitches removed in about the same amount of days. Lamar's wound is large. He needs to keep it bandaged and clean since many of the villagers have AIDS. The lab test's show that, Lamar, doesn't have HIV, but he still must have the information needed to protect himself "forever" from getting it. Educating him at his age is of utmost importance."

Appy explained to Brent what Dr. Sarah had just said.

"I'm so happy for my son. I know my wife will cry tears of joy. We've had many educational talks with him already. Certainly, we'll continue."

Throughout the visit with Dr. Sarah, Appy glanced at her several times. Dr. Sarah, also, looked his way more than once. Her hair was dark brown with an auburn cast to it. She had it pulled back and held at the back of her neck with a hair clip. She possessed brilliant blue eyes that seemed to twinkle like stars in the night with a skin complexion that was fair and rosy. Of course, he didn't overlook her hourglass figure and sensual lips—all of which made her stunning to him. *"Wow,"* Appy thought to himself. *"She's amazingly my kind of girl."*

He never found himself interested in any girls at St. Matthew or in college for that matter. This attraction was a different experience for him—much different.

On the way back, Rahl took Brent and Lamar home first, so that Lamar could rest.

"We'll be back in ten days," Appy said. "You'll be itching by then to get those stitches out, Lamar."

Appy shook Brent's hand. He also extended his hand to, Lamar. Lamar shook Appy's hand smiling at the acknowledgment.

Both Rahl and Appy said together, "b*onsoir*."

"At least," Rahl said, "I now know how to say good day and good evening in French."

"Yeah, journalist, you're making progress," Appy chuckled.

When Rahl and Appy reached Sisters of Amity, most of the children were in school. It gave Appy an opportunity to help Father Reed with his computer without interference.

Father Reed commented, "Oh Appy, I'm so thrilled with your ability to repair these machines."

Appy set up an account with a wireless network using Father Reed's credit card to activate his service. The two sat down and Appy reacquainted Father Reed with e-mail and news.

"Father, you'll need more assistance, but it takes more than one day. I'll be in Nairi for a long while, so we'll get through this."

"I'm so grateful, Appy. Take this money, its well deserved."

"Thank you, Father. I can use a little spending money. I bought some cookies for the children on Father Jeff's dime when Rahl and I went to the post office and grocery store in town. I need to pay him back for the goodies. When I get back, I'll have Father Jeff e-mail you, so check your computer tonight."

"Oh, sounds exciting, Appy, I'll check out the news today, as well."

Appy excused himself and walked into the big room. He grabbed his mat and placed it in the center of the room while Sister Myra stood a distance away to see how the children would react. Appy opened his cookie bag. He handed Zenna and Jimi each one.

"Here you are Zenna." "Here you are Jimi."

The other younger toddlers came stumbling as fast as they could forward with their mats. As anticipated, the tots were popping off their names.

"I Ukita," "I Tobi."

Appy regarded Sister Myra with a smile. He gave each a cookie that said their name. The shy toddlers wondered why they hadn't received a cookie and looked very puzzled. Appy walked around a little—then turned back to give them their share. Tobi was eating his own delicious cookie while eyeing Ukita's cookie to see if she'd share her treat with him, too. Ukita rolled her eyes upward letting him know, "Not a chance bud!"

While regarding Ukita, Appy chuckled, "You tots are hilarious!"

Sister Myra remarked, "Appy you're a natural born teacher."

"I never acquired the credentials for that, Sister. But—I hope to make a good daddy someday."

Sarah's face suddenly flashed before him. Just then, Rahl and Father Reed entered the room. "Ap, do you think we should head back to see how Father Jeff is doing with Ladi and the pups?"

Rahl had told Father Reed already about the experience that made him "grandpa."

"When we come back Father, we'll bring the pups, so the children can enjoy them. It'll give them an opportunity to be gentle with little animals."

"Sure, that's fine with me."

Appy also told Father Reed, "I've written the Sisters at St. Matthew about sending baseball equipment. I'll use the money you gave me to send them for postage fees."

"It's possible, Appy, that I may get the contributors of the mission to pay for that. They should be grateful for the free mitts and baseball bats. Without a doubt though, if these children were going to stay here in Nairi, their preference would probably be football; but because the children are mostly going back to the States for adoption, they should be acquainted with baseball, as well. It'll be a new experience for them."

Appy continued, "Once we move into Sisters of Amity, I'll begin to gather the older boys and girls to start the training of rules. I forgot to ask Sister Jenny to send me a book on baseball rules, but she's so smart, Father Reed; she may do that without me asking."

"You think a great deal of, Sister Jenny?" Father Reed asked.

"She has been my mentor all my life. I think she's what a mother would be like."

"As head of Sisters of Amity's home, Appy, that's good to know. If only all orphans with a lesser chance of adoption because of their age or sex, had someone like Sister Jenny to support them, turn out a man like you, we'd all be blessed."

"At times, Father, I deal with feelings of abandonment, but I've learned that we all have insecurities in our lives. Still, I want to thank you for that fine compliment."

Father Reed made another astute remark, "I also feel that some people are born with a keen sense of reasonableness. I think that of you, Appy."

"Wow, Father, that's good of you to say."

CHAPTER 3

After dinner at the mission house, Father Jeff said, "How about we get to the business of naming these pups?"

"Okay," replied Rahl. "We should write names on paper. Each put down one that'd fit a girl and one that'd fit a boy. If we don't agree on names right off, we can write more until we're in agreement."

Father Jeff read off the first set of names, "Let me see there is Wade, Clyde, and Biff, for the guy names—Grace, Tiny, and Keena for the gal names. I like, Biff."

"I do, too." Appy agreed.

"Well, that's three for three," Rahl declared. "So we have a, Biff."

"For the girl, I put down, Grace," said Father Jeff, "but I think I like Keena better."

All agreed on, Keena. Rahl, happily announced, "Well, we have a Biff and a Keena—so cute."

Father Jeff asked, "I wonder, Rahl, if Ruthy will be upset that she had no say in naming these pups?"

"Hell no," Rahl said, "She doesn't warm up to any animals. She puts up with Ladi because I care about her so much. Being fair to

Ruthy, occasionally I see her pet Ladi when she comes around her. Ruthy never had pets because of her allergies. She doesn't seem to miss them either. Animals were just never a consideration in her life. If she had had an animal around her when she was a youngster, she may have built up immunities to these allergies, but I'm no doctor. What do I know?"

"By the way, Father," Appy said, "I told Father Reed to check his computer for a message from you."

"Okay, I better start now since I'm just a one finger typist."

Hi Father Reed,

This is so wonderful! I watched the news today, did you? I also played the game solitaire. I liked it—tells my age. We've named the pups Biff and Keena. I just love their puppy breath! Ladi is an excellent mother. If you send a message back, we'll know we're in business. We'll be hoping to hear from you. Father Jeff

Hello everyone,

I received your message, Father Jeff. Yes, this is so wonderful. I can't tell you how thrilled I am. If you're ready to move in here, we're ready for you. I like the names that you gave the pups. I hope that Rahl will visit us much, so we can enjoy Ladi's pups, as well as, Ladi. A pediatrician named Dr. Sarah Henderson is coming to examine the children at the end of this week. She's an intern in pediatrics volunteering her service to Sisters of Amity—a very busy girl to be so charitable. We're very grateful. We can all help her gather up and keep the children calm through these examinations.

Father Reed

Appy excitingly said, "Wow, Rahl, do you think he's talking about the same Dr. Sarah we met at the hospital?"

"Sure sounds like it, I'd say?"

Appy's heart was pounding.

"Ap," Rahl said. "You seem taken with this girl."

"Oh gosh, I think that she's really someone I could fall for. I could not speak I was so drawn to her. How the heck do you get a girl to go on a date if you can't speak?"

Rahl teased, "Maybe she's coming to the home to see you again since I said you were going to live at Sisters of Amity."

"Oh, take that back, Rahl, because now I'll be really nervous around her."

"Here's a tip Ap, let her ask questions, you answer them. Then when your nervousness is over, you'll be able to carry on a conversation."

"What's this about, Appy?" Father Jeff asked.

"Nothing yet Father," answered Appy, "but should I get a chance to woo her, it could be a romance like no other. I will say it's difficult for me to date a girl with no job, no money, and no car."

Father laughed, "True."

"What do you think, Appy? Should we go tomorrow to Sisters of Amity to set up our rooms?"

"Okay Father, if Rahl can drive us, I'm game." *"I'm really game!"* He thought to himself.

"Sure, but I'll miss you guys. Who'll make meals for me or share the dust in my jeep?"

"Yuk, fat chance we'll miss that, Rahl," answered Appy. "When is Ruthy coming back?" Appy asked.

"She will be here in about five days. I hope to have everyone over for dinner, so that she can be acquainted with everyone. Ruthy is a good cook. She cooks a mean roast and potato combo."

"That sounds terrific, Rahl," Father Jeff said, "I can smell it—now. Moreover, anytime you want a meal, you can come over and spend time with us."

"I may take you up on that, Father," Rahl answered.

"Please come for lunch often," Appy replied, "because we'll be missing you, Ladi, Keena, and Biff very much."

Father Jeff and Appy packed some things the night before; the two finished packing in the morning.

Appy asked Father Jeff, "Did you remember to bring our bug spray?"

"Yes, I did."

"Have you noticed, Father, that there are fewer flies at Sisters of Amity than at the village?"

"Oh yes, for sure," Father Jeff answered, "They're bigger, too."

"Brent told me," Appy continued, "that the waste that exists at the village is burned, but not frequent enough."

"Appy, would you please fetch me a bucket of water? I want to bathe, Ladi. A nursing mother needs to keep clean. The children will be around her. I can just wash the pups faces and paws. Maybe we can throw a sheet over them for the dusty ride."

Rahl said, "I'll raise the jeep's top. We shouldn't get so much dust, besides it isn't so windy today."

Father Jeff continuing with small talk, "We're fortunate to have a shaft for water next to the mission house. I wonder if the village has one."

"Yes," answered Rahl. "The Nairi government drilled several shafts, so the people could exist. There's also one at Sisters of Amity."

Rahl said, "When you finish bathing and drying, Ladi, we'll eat and then hit the dusty trail."

"Rahl, give me a hand loading up these computers that aren't working—I'll take them to Sisters of Amity for repair."

"Okay, Ap, I'll be right with you."

"Wow," Father Jeff bragged. "These doggies are clean and smell so good!" Rahl asked the men "Are you ready to load up?"

After piling the luggage in and Ladi with pups placed in the jeep, the men jumped in and off they went. The pups, most often robust, were calm in the jeep, and kept sucking on, mom.

Rahl pulled up to the clergy house. Father Reed was there to greet them.

"Hi gentlemen, this will be an exciting day. Please come this way. I'll show you your rooms."

"Oh, this is fine," Father Jeff, said.

"Yes, it's just great," Appy, agreed. Appy asked Father Reed, "Do you have anything like a shed where I can put these computers to work on them?"

"Yes," Father Reed answered. "There's a shed in the back that has a makeshift workbench that might work for you. I'll take you there, later."

Appy said, "That'll be fine."

Rahl brought Ladi and the pups in the big room. He put them on a rug inside a good size cage that Father Reed had, so as not to relieve themselves on the children's mats or floor. When Appy walked in, the toddlers came unsteadily toward him.

Rahl said, "You're a popular guy around here, Ap."

Tobi carried his rug and Appy's to the center of the room.

"Thank you, Tobi," Appy said.

Even more toddlers came forward with names this time. After giving out cookies, Appy took the pups out. Everyone watched them bounce and run. Puppy Keena thought Jimi's toe was something else. Jimi scooted his rug back just far enough to up himself. He ran to, Sister Myra.

He pointed at puppy Keena saying, "Bad."

Sister Myra replied, "No, puppy Keena isn't bad. She's a baby."

Jimi repeated, "Babee."

"You see, Jimi," Sister Myra in a teaching moment said, "the baby pups get milk from their mother's nipples just like you get milk from a bottle with a nipple on it. The baby puppy thought your little toe was a nipple. When that happens again, just push her away gently."

Jimi went over to puppy, Keena, and pushed her a little. Sister Myra and Appy laughed.

"He's practicing," Appy said. "These toddlers amuse me to no end."

Appy picked up Keena putting her back in her cage to feed. He then went to attend to a crying baby. He sat in the rocker giving him his bottle.

The toddler Zenna began trying to impress, Appy. She said with her hand on her chest, "Watch Zenna dance," "Watch Zenna dance!" She tapped her toes and whirled her arms in the air. Of course, Zenna didn't know much about dance, but Appy thought her moves looked good.

"At three, Zenna, you're the cutest little tyke. Come here and I'll kiss you on your forehead." She did.

Appy was burping the baby when Father Reed came in.

"Lunch is ready. How about you, Sister Myra, would you like to eat with us?"

"No thank you, Father. You're taking my best helper. I need to keep a watch on these toddlers until Sister Clare comes in from the schoolhouse."

"Oh," said Appy. "If nobody makes me do dishes, I'll be back to help you out."

"Good," said Sister Myra. "I'll appreciate that."

When lunch was over and school let out, Sister Clare brought the older children in. Some were very helpful with the little ones—diapering, carrying, and one that even sang to them.

"Sister Clare," Appy said. "That girl sings beautifully."

"Yes, her name is, Sadie. She's only thirteen. She lost her parents to AIDS. Fortunately, she wasn't infected. We were able to take her here. Her talent is overlooked here, but she might have a chance as an adult with that singing voice."

"Wow, Sister, that's a shame."

"It's a shame for every one of them." Sister Myra remarked. "She came from a middle class family, but AIDS doesn't spare anybody because of their means or education."

"Sister Clare," Appy said. "I need to get these older children together to go over baseball rules with them. I need them to help the younger children. I'm only one person and need some assistance. I'd like to see them after school out on the field. The cooks and I will make up some peanut butter and jelly sandwiches with some flavored water drinks. I definitely will need their attention for about two hours, both boys and girls."

"It's good to hear the girls are included," Sister Clare stated. "Oftentimes, people think we can't be good at sports."

"Sister Clare?" Appy said. "I wouldn't think of letting the girls have their own team. Surely they'd skunk us guys every game, but never mind telling the boys I said that. At the home where I lived, the girls were awesome at baseball."

Father Reed came into the gathering room. He asked Appy, "Are you and Rahl ready to put those computers in the shed?"

"Sure," Appy answered. "I'm anxious to set up a workshop."

"Yes," Rahl seconded, "I should go back soon before the sun sets. I'm thinking of stopping by the village to check on, Lamar."

Appy said with concern, "Okay Rahl that sounds good. By the way, when you take Lamar to get his stitches removed, I want to go with you. I'd like to see Brent and Lamar again."

"And I'd think Dr. Sarah too," Rahl teased.

"Well, her too," Appy answered with a robust smile.

Rahl went for his jeep. He pulled it up to the shed.

"Father Reed," Appy said. "This shed is perfect. That bench and stool will give me the space I need to repair these computers. I need to get one working for Father Jeff. I'll try to get him international service, so that he can communicate with St. Matthew. I know he misses the children that he has grown so close to."

A half-hour later, Rahl left Sisters of Amity. Moreover, Appy organized his shed. He thought that early morning hours with coffee in hand would be a good time to work on the machines. That would give him time to be with the youngsters before the older children are out of school. He thought to himself, "I *can also store the bats and mitts in here.*"

After school, Sister Clare had the children out on the field.

"Boys and girls," Appy said. "I'm sure you've seen me around here lately. My name is Appy and tomorrow I'd like you to tape your names and ages on your clothing. I know you might think that childish at your age, but you only have my name to remember. On the other hand, I have many names to learn. "Sadie," Appy requested, "You sing beautifully—would you please come over here by me." As she neared him, he asked her, "Would you mind if I appoint you to sing the National Anthem of Nairi before all games?"

Sadie answered, "Okay, thank you, sir."

"Please call me, Appy, or, Ap. That goes for everybody."

"Now step around me," Appy said in a loud voice. "Every one of you will be team helpers for the little six through eleven-year-olds who need you to teach and root for them. Girls, we need about five cheerleaders to make cheers—think about it, and let me know the day after tomorrow. The game baseball is new to you. I'll teach you the rules. You need to respect these young ones as if each is the most important person on the field. These are some rules for you to keep in mind, I) to be instructors on the game, 2) to make a point of learning everyone's name, 3) offer water and request that they drink it to stay hydrated. If anyone refuses, come tell me, 4) I want you to love these little people, as I will respect you for doing so. Finally, laugh with them often, but never belittle them on their errors—just inform them, 'You'll do better tomorrow.' They need to know competition, but not in a way that crushes them."

"First things first," Appy continued, "I'm an orphan who was never adopted. Therefore, I know your pain. I, also, know we need each other. You can come to me if you need someone to talk with. This is my favorite game. I'm very familiar with it. I hope you like it as I do. Sister Myra is going to be my assistant coach. I need a scorekeeper. Who's good at math?" Everyone pointed to, Jayla.

Appy requested, "Jayla, if it's all right with you, will you be my scorekeeper?"

"Sure, I can do that, Ap," Jayla answered.

Appy said with strength, "Okay, we'll begin to play. I will pitch; each one of you will bat. If you hit the ball, you'll run to the old mats that Sister Myra gave us as bases. There are three bases and home base here where I am standing. For now, we can practice that much."

To Appy's amazement, the first batter up hit the ball way out in left field. Appy said cheerfully, "Now, you know why we need outfielders."

"I'll get that ball," said a boy running toward outfield.

"What's your name?" Appy hollered.

"My name is Gbandi."

"Okay, Gbandi, stay out there. I'll send two more out there the next time we play because we need one right fielder, one center fielder, and one left fielder."

Gbandi hollered back, "Get, Chikae, to work the right side for now."

Appy called out, "Okay, Chikae, where are you? Go out with Gbandi only on the opposite side of the field."

The batting went well. Everyone seemed to be excited about the game. First, second, and third basemen were set up. All balls thrown to bases were grounders because there weren't enough mitts to go around. The boys and girls played well. Each seemed to have a good time. They ate sandwiches while laughing back and forth at some of their plays.

"You guys and gals can do that with each other, but not around the youngsters. Remember…every young child will want to be great and cry easily. I don't know about any of you, but I'm not sure I can handle that."

While crinkling their noses, they commented, "Me neither!" "Me neither!"

Appy mentioned, "Tomorrow, Dr. Sarah is coming to Sisters of Amity. We'll all be busy, so the next day we'll play. Everyone line up—slap the hand of the teammate next to you. Now slap mine, thank you! Did you have fun?"

All agreed by clapping their hands in a musical manner.

"Having fun gals and gents is the most important feature of baseball."

The session ended with all walking away talking and discussing the rules of the game. Appy and Sister Myra were very happy with the whole day.

Appy thought to himself, *"For children with absolutely no knowledge of how to play baseball, they tried so hard, did so well."*

The group pulled together and seemed to bond nicely with each other.

CHAPTER 4

The next day, Dr. Sarah and the nurses pulled up at Sisters of Amity. The men shook her hand. She introduced them to the nurses.

"Well," she said. "I remember Rahl and Appy. Have you heard how the boy's wound is doing?"

"Not yet," Appy answered. "Rahl was going to stop there last evening. He said he'd let me know sometime today." Appy thought, *"Rahl was right about answering Sarah's questions."* It helped break the quietness that he'd been experiencing around her.

Sarah said, "Sister Myra told me that the older children will be playing a game that could cause wounds. If you men will line up and comfort the patients, my nurses will give the older ones their tetanus shot."

"That shows me just what a good assistant coach Sister Myra will be," Appy replied.

The teens, aware that Appy was near, kept themselves restrained and calm since they wouldn't want him thinking they were babies. Appy went down the line and slapped each of his players on the hand.

"What does that mean?" asked Dr. Sarah.

Appy answered, "It's something we do to acknowledge each other in baseball line up."

Dr. Sarah looked down the long line, "Okay, here we go."

Those who got their shots encouraged the others.

"Nothing to it," Gbandi and Chikae said.

Two children needed vaccinations. Dr. Sarah informed Appy that this area needed to remain clean, and that the area would most likely be sore and scab over.

After that, Dr. Sarah said, "Appy we need to give each toddler one shot."

"Oh gosh, that's going to break my heart," Appy moaned.

"I have a little numbing medicine that I can spray on the little ones topically before injecting them. Appy hold the first child," Dr. Sarah said quietly.

"Oh, Zenna, I'm so sorry," Appy, sighed.

It was over very fast. Appy carried her to get a cookie. With tears flooding her cheeks, she still ate her cookie.

Appy said to the teens, "Please hold the little ones until they want down."

He helped with all the other toddlers. He said to Dr. Sarah, "I am exhausted emotionally. They're too precious to hurt like this."

"We don't want them getting childhood diseases that could take their lives," Dr. Sarah answered.

Father Jeff and Father Reed seemed affected, as well.

Father Jeff said, "They're capable of handling this situation."

"Yes," said Father Reed. "Let's go and have a piece of cake."

The injections were soon over. Dr. Sarah and Appy sat down while the nurses cleaned the area up.

"I understand you do computer repair."

"Yes, my degree is in Electrical Engineering. When I leave Africa, I'll be looking for work in manufacturing, repairing, designing, and improving computers."

"You know," Sarah, said, "there's a message board at the hospital. They're looking for a person that's excellent in electronics preferring someone with computer repair skills. But, I believe it said only part-time seekers need apply."

"Part-time would be great! I'm here in Nairi to experience Africa before I pursue my career at home. Rahl and I will be bringing Lamar back to have his stitches removed. I'll check that out then."

"Dr. Sarah, come and see the shed that Father Reed has loaned me to work on computers."

"Sure," she politely answered. "Wow!"

The desktops were all operating—looking very colorful with many different backgrounds.

"I haven't asked anyone else, not even the Fathers, to come and see this display, yet. I'll check my e-mail while I'm here. Yep, Rahl has left an e-mail. Let me check this out while you're here. He says that Lamar's stitches look good. The pups are cute as ever. He also wants to know how our day went today. I'll e-mail him back tonight."

As if out of nowhere, Appy asked, "Are you married, Dr. Sarah?"

"No, no, I'm not. I've been too busy with 2½ years to go on my internship. I've been on one date in the last four years."

"Oh girl, I'd love to be your second date."

Sarah blushed, "If you drop the Doctor title, I might take you up on that."

Appy chuckled, "I need to get that job first."

Both laughed.

"However, I'm dead serious about that date."

Appy was proud of himself—that he made his intentions very clear. The nurses were waiting at Dr. Sarah's car. They said their good-byes. Appy went back to the shed. He thought he'd e-mail Rahl.

Hi Rahl,

Your suggestion about only answering questions, worked out well. I had a great day. I asked her out on a date! I'm going to look into a job at the hospital that Sarah mentioned to me. When we go to take Lamar's stitches out, I will check with human resources there. As you can see, she said I'd have to drop the "Doctor" title. She seems to like me, too. I am glad to hear that Ladi, Keena, and Biff are doing well. Father Jeff has no idea that all the computers that needed repair are fixed. The desktop colors and pictures are all different. Sarah seemed impressed. I tried everything! Is Ruthy coming in soon? Since I have no money, I'd like to ask Sarah to come to a baseball game to see the boys and girls of Sisters of Amity at their very best. It'd be nice for you and Ruthy to come, too, so we can get the girls acquainted.

Also, Rahl, there's a lot of chain link fencing in the back of the shed. I'd like to get 4-8 foot galvanized poles and two bags of cement. The boys and I will build a protective fence for spectators— Sisters, toddlers, and guests. It'll also protect players that are waiting on the bench. These teen boys and girls are just great. You should see how excited they are! I'm not even married, yet. Still, I want to adopt them all. What's the matter with people; they're precious people coming into adulthood needing only one thing—love? Get back with me soon. Ap

Appy went back to the home. He helped Sister Myra and Sister Clare with preparing the children for bed.

"How's your boo boo, Zenna?"

She replied, "Zenna, dance tomorrow."

"Okay, Sweetheart, let me help you brush your teeth." Appy thought, "*This little girl has my heart!*" Finding himself quite tired, he also went to bed early.

After a good night's rest, he was up early the next day working the newly repaired computers. They were working very well. He checked out the weather and news for the day. Nairi called for rain. He thought that would be wonderful. Father Jeff usually woke up at eight o'clock every morning.

Appy went back to the residence saying, "Father Jeff, grab your coffee. Come with me."

"What's this, a surprise party?"

"Oh yes, something similar to that." When Father Jeff entered the shed, his eyes lit up, his mouth dropped.

"My goodness, Appy, you're amazing."

"Father, this computer is for you. All we have to do is set up an account with international services. You'll then be able to connect with St. Matthew. It'll cost a little more per month, but not much more. I can do this for you now. You'll be set to go."

"That'd be wonderful, Appy," said Father Jeff. "I miss everybody so much. I can talk to some of the children. Some had birthdays that I've missed. I wonder if Father Larry is scooping ice cream on cones weekly. You know the children just loved seeing me come in to serve them their ice cream cones."

"Oh, I know very well, Father. On those days when you came in to scoop ice cream, I felt like you were my, daddy. Pretty much you were. Oh yes, Father Jeff, you definitely need this service to put your mind at ease while giving you much enjoyment...."

"Set it up, Appy. I never spend much money on myself. As you said, I'll receive so much enjoyment when corresponding with St. Matthew. I'm excited!"

Appy mentioned, "...Not exactly a party, but nevertheless a surprise just for you."

Father Jeff hugged, Appy. He cupped his hand on his shoulder.

"I don't know what a son is anymore than you know what parents are, Ap. But you're the closest image I have of having a real son."

Tears welled in both men's eyes.

That time spent with Father Jeff made the whole day beautiful for Appy. Appy went to the big room to enjoy the babies and toddlers. He sat on the rocker in the center of the floor. He watched the toddlers gather their rugs. They sat down next to him. The toddlers seemed to know it was to early for goodies. The young ones sat there chatting away with each other, seeming to understand the babble of all.

"*How funny,*" Appy thought to himself.

Zenna came over saying, "I wuve Pap Pee."

Appy smiled, "I love you, too, Zenna."

While sitting in the big room tending to the kiddies, Appy was drafting his re`sume`. In it, he stressed that he didn't need much more than part-time work, preferring to repair the computers in his workshop at Sisters of Amity. He'd be able to pick up the computers that were down and return them to the hospital when repaired. He could also spend one day in the hospital servicing computers that had crashed or had a virus. Of course, he went into his credentials, education, and such.

Father Reed came in and Appy asked him, "May I use your typewriter today Father, so that my re`sume` looks a little more professional?"

"Sure, I'll get it from my bedroom. Maybe you could bring it in your shed to type without so many distractions."

"Yes, the workbench will be good for that. When I'm out there, come out and see my workshop. I think you'll be surprised."

"Okay," Father Reed said. "I'll do that."

Appy waited until naptime. He handed out mats, blankets and pillows. The children lay on their mats, closed their eyes, and at least rested.

Sister Myra said to, Appy, "Eventually they'll go off."

Appy slipped away with Father Reed's typewriter to his work area. He was just finishing his one page re'sume' when Father Reed came into the shed.

"Wow, Appy, you're going places. Are you aware that your talent is going to bring you a handsome living one day?" Father Reed stated.

Appy said proudly, "This computer is for Father Jeff. He can now e-mail St. Matthew."

Father Reed asked, "Is Father Jeff going to bring it to his bedroom? I can have the Sisters look for a desk of sorts. In fact, we have a sewing machine that sits in a nice cabinet. The lid on the cabinet would make for a nice desktop. We can look for a chair and Father Jeff will be all set."

"I'll help you do that, Father Reed. Then, Father Jeff will have some privacy in his own room."

"Appy everybody has been very much bored around here for a long time. You have opened the outside world to us, again."

"When I return home Father Reed, all you have to do is send me your problem computers. I'll ship them back repaired."

"That's so reassuring, Appy. Thank you."

"Father Reed I'd like Gbandi and Chikae to work with me. The time is now while they're young to teach them about repairing these machines. They're the oldest boys here needing good skills for adulthood."

"Of course, Father Reed said. "They'll be delighted to join you."

When Appy and Sister Myra met the teens on the field, it began to rain. The rain was of a very fine texture with no thunder or lightening.

Appy said, "Look at that rainbow with its magnificent colors, a beautiful sight."

He raised his face and hands into the rain—shouting, "Get out in the rain. Enjoy yourself! A cooling rain doesn't happen here often."

Everyone was having such fun when the sun popped out and the rain stopped.

Appy said, "Okay, come and have a sandwich and drink. It should give everyone energy to play a good game. That two-minute rain just didn't last long enough."

He also passed out an apple to each. It wasn't an easy job putting twenty sandwiches together, but Sister Myra and the cooks helped.

"Today," Coach Appy said, "we'll make up teams, team one and team two, and you'll learn more if we just play. When the mitts and bats come in, our fun will be over. Then we'll need to teach the younger boys and girls the game. This has proven to be so much fun with every one of you. In the future, we'll have special games just for us."

This game was surely exciting! The cheerleaders headed by Sadie did a terrific job. They apparently got together with Sister Clare and came up with some good cheers. The cheerleaders had to play also to make up team count. The game ended with Jayla giving fifteen runs to team one, fourteen runs to team two.

Appy said all pumped up, "Good job! I hope everyone had fun."

Everybody lined up; the hand slapping was a bit louder. Appy felt that the teens had a good time. They seemed to be into the game.

"Gbandi—Chikae, I'd like to talk with the two of you," Appy said quietly.

Both gathered around him. Appy began to tell them, "Since I may get a job at the hospital, I'd like to teach you two how to repair computers. I need your help with these repairs. In five years, you'll be nineteen. This skill could help you make a good living someday."

Both boys were puffed-up. Each was equally excited about Appy's proposal.

Smiling from ear to ear Gbandi said, "We'll do our best."

"That's all I ask," Appy, answered.

CHAPTER 5

Rahl e-mailed Appy the night before that he'd come his way first at about one o'clock. Together they'd pick up Brent and Lamar before heading to the hospital. Appy, dressed nicely. He hoped Rahl would put the jeeps top up. He picked up his re`sume`, folded it, and put it in his pocket. He was thrilled to get a chance to see Sarah again. He was also missing Rahl, Brent, and Lamar.

An hour later Rahl pulled up, "What do you have there, Rahl?"

Extended over the whole jeep's right side were 4-8 foot poles with two bags of cement in the rear of the jeep.

Appy shook Rahl's hand, "You're a good friend."

As the two pulled the poles off the jeep to place them behind the shed, "What do I owe you, Rahl?"

"This is my gift to the children. You're not the only good guy around Africa."

"Rahl, that's so good of you. I know you'll feel proud every time you watch a game seeing how much the children enjoy being together in play."

"Ap—Ruthy and I can come and help build the fence this Friday. She's very good with fences. She can't do the heavy labor, but she knows how to do it. Her father owns a fencing business."

"Oh wow, life couldn't be better for me, Rahl. Do you think we could put the top up on the jeep? I dressed up for this job interview, also for Sarah's approval."

"Sure, I'm happy for you, a possible job and a gal, too. What the hell, no wonder your life is so good?"

"I do hope my luck holds since I'm asking to repair these machines in my workshop. Maybe spend one day at the hospital putting in new connections. I never want to be so super involved that I can't help Father Jeff with the decisions he has to make. To bring twelve children home, we need to do a lot of soul searching. I'll accept a little less in pay if that can be agreed upon."

Father Jeff came out front. He handed Appy two reference letters, one from him and one from, Father Reed.

"Thank you," Appy said in a mellow voice. "Thank you, very much."

The two put the jeep top up. They were off to pick up Brent and Lamar.

"Rahl, how are the pups doing?"

"Fine, I think you should take one once they're weaned."

Appy said thoughtfully, "I'll think about that, but I need to discuss this with Father Jeff and Father Reed. After all, it isn't like I pay rent here, so I must have a consensus on that before it happens."

Lamar came running out toward the jeep, "*salute, comment allezvous?*"

Appy replied, "Okay."

Brent came out smiling while buttoning his shirt.

"Tell—Brent," Rahl said. "That we can shop in town while you do your interview."

Appy interpreted for Brent what Rahl had said. Brent held up his finger in a gesture to wait. He went to get some more money from his wife.

"Shopping will be great," Brent said cheerfully.

"Rahl, how do you think Brent will do with the language barrier?"

"I have a feeling that he knows how to handle that. When it comes to money, people learn those words fast."

"You're probably right," agreed Appy.

At the hospital, Dr. Sarah came in.

"How's everything going?"

"Well, your patient Lamar is doing fine, but I need to leave. I'm going to human resources to see about that job."

"Go ahead; it only takes two minutes to take the stitches out. I hope Lamar will forgive my lack of French."

61

Rahl broke in, "The rest of us are going to do a little shopping in town, so after, we'll circle around back to pick Ap up."

"Is that what you call him, Rahl? I like that!"

Appy bowed, "Sarah, I give you permission to call me that."

"Okay, Ap, it'll be."

"Well, here goes; wish me luck."

Rahl said, "Go get 'em friend."

Sarah did a thumb up, "Give Mr. Cronc your best."

"Sarah, I'll return here. I need to talk with you."

"Okay, Ap."

Appy, winked at her as he whispered. "It's about our date."

Sarah's cheekbones raised in a big knowing smile as she made known, "I'm here all day."

Mr. Cronc in human resources was very impressed with, Appy. Having two established priests backing him helped enormously. He gave Appy a list of company rules.

"You'll have medical insurance with this hospital and with our doctors. In addition, as long as your work is good, you can bring the computers to Sisters of Amity. Of course, we need you to sign these machines out, how many machines, how many parts, and so forth."

"Of course, I realize, Mr. Cronc, you don't know me. I hope to gain your trust over time. As I said before, I'll be here for two years. I'm also training two boys that you might want to hire when I leave."

"Because of your situation," Mr. Cronc said, "I'm giving you an advance on your pay."

Appy, thought to himself, "*What did the Fathers' write?*"

Whatever they wrote Appy was grateful. The two shook hands. Appy left. He went back to Sarah's office to speak with her.

"Sarah, I'm having a baseball game on Friday at Sisters of Amity. I thought you might enjoy coming. We will be grilling hot dogs with chips and drinks. Rahl and his girl friend Ruthy will also be there. I've never met Ruthy, so we'll both be meeting her for the first time. We're going to put up a fence earlier in the day before the game. I hope to have the younger children watch the game, as well. Do you have a computer, Sarah?"

"Yes, I do."

"Could I have your e-mail address? I promise not to stalk you," he chuckled.

"Sure, I'll also need your's, Ap, just in case something awful comes up, but I'll make every effort to come to the game. By the way Ap, did you get the job?"

"Oh yes, I did."

"That's great!" Sarah said pleasingly. She came close and hugged him.

"*Oh, gee!*" Appy thought to himself, "I *want her to hold me...* *forever.*"

"Well, my beeper's going off. I need to return to work. You have my e-mail address. Write me, Ap."

She walked him to the door and hurried down the corridor. Appy went to the rear parking lot to wait for, Rahl. When Rahl drove up, the jeep looked about half-full.

"Rahl, I need to go around back and pick up some computers."

"You got the job?"

"Yes, I did!"

"Ap this is so exciting. Hop in, we'll go get them."

Appy told Brent about his job. Brent patted him on the back. Once the computers were loaded, Rahl drove back through town. At the edge of the town, there was a fruit vendor.

"Stop here, Rahl," Appy shouted.

He leaped out of the jeep and bought two-bushel baskets of apples.

Rahl said, "We're loaded now. We need to head home."

On the way home, Appy explained to Brent that he'd like Lamar to play baseball with the children at Sisters of Amity. I need to train someone to be umpire of all the games. It's an important position. I'd like to see Lamar in that spot.

Lamar piped in, "*oui, je voudrais que*, Papa."

"As you can understand, my son likes the idea."

"There's an old car behind Father Reed's shed that supposedly doesn't work. I'd like to look it over to see if it's just something minor, maybe a sensor chip that needs replacing. That wouldn't take much time to fix. Father Reed said, it'd run—but then, just stop running in the middle of the road. Makes me believe it's shorting out."

Rahl asked, "Are you also in mechanics?"

"When I was in high school, I took it for three years. I'm rather good at it. The Fathers let me work on their cars. If I get that car up and running Brent, I could pick Lamar up myself. Otherwise, I need to rely on you, Rahl."

"I've never minded, Ap. That's why I'm here to relate with the people and feel their life in my soul."

"By the way Rahl, have you used your computer to document your notes, lately? It looks like everyone is going to have a place in your magazine piece, so I want you to take good notes."

"Oh yes," Rahl chuckled, "I have you down as the computer nerd." Appy, laughed robustly. He let Brent and Lamar know why he was laughing so hardily.

Appy said to Brent, "Friday we're having a game. You and your family are invited. We'll be serving hot dogs from the grill with potato chips and some drinks. Do you have a relief person Brent that can take over when you're gone?"

"Oh, yes I do," Brent, answered

"Do you have a computer?"

"I do, but it needs repair."

"When we get to the village, have Lamar bring it out. I'll look it over."

Rahl placed his arm over Appy's seat, "Father Jeff once said to me that, 'You're an expert.' He's so right."

Appy asked Brent, "Will the Nairi government pay for the service?"

Brent assured him, "When it was working, they did."

"Rahl it's hard to believe so many computers are down in these parts."

"Not enough people are skilled in repairing them, Ap. It costs more to repair the damn things than to buy a new one."

"But, Rahl, there's not that much wrong with them."

"Oh Ap, for owners who know nothing about repairing these digital wizards, it's just plain damn irritating and overwhelming."

When they dropped off Brent and Lamar, Appy pulled out one-bushel basket of apples. Brent, please pass these out to the children.

"*Merci* b*eaucoup*," Brent replied.

"Lamar, we'll wait here for your papa's computer."

Lamar soon came out with the computer and parts, "au revoir." He said.

"Ap, friend, you're one-bushel basket of apples ahead of me on the goodness scale. I need to catch up."

Upon returning, Appy went out into the shed. He worked a couple hours on the computers he was given. Later, he stopped by Father Jeff's room. He was on his computer composing a letter to St. Matthew.

"Let me shut this down, Appy. How did it go?"

"Well, I was hired. Mr. Cronc also gave me an advance in pay."

"Oh gosh, that's so good to hear. I've worried and wondered all day about whether you were successful or not."

Appy thought, "I *should have come right in to tell, Father.*"

"Good news, Father. I landed the deal I wanted. I'll be able to do the repairs here—only go to the hospital one day a week to reconnect the repaired computers. They're paying me a weekly salary, paid every two weeks with full benefits. Once I prove myself, the pay will increase considerably."

Appy informed Father Jeff that he asked Sarah to come to Sisters of Amity for Friday's game.

"Rahl is going to pick up hot dogs, chips, and some flavored drinks. I, also, bought 2 bushel baskets of apples, but I gave one to Brent for the children in the village."

"I'd also like to join in that, Appy. Please count me in when you buy for the village. I'd rather get ice cream and make cones," Father said. "However, that wouldn't work with the long drive out here. You can tell Rahl to buy bags of cookies that the children will enjoy—chocolate cookies! Of course, I'll pay him when he gets here."

"How did things go with, Dr. Sarah?"

"I think she's going to be my girl. The attraction seems mutual. She hugged me today when she heard I got the job. The hair on my arms stood straight up from the goose bumps I had."

Father Jeff thoughtfully said, "Do I need to sit down and have a talk with you about the opposite sex, Appy?"

"Oh no, please...you only know how to be celibate."

Both men laughed.

"I'm beginning to sound like, Rahl. He's always so funny. I noticed being around priests my whole life, I never swear like other men."

They both laughed again.

"Rahl is a fine man in his heart. I know we'll be friends, forever. I guess I'll go see the toddlers for a while. I love that little, Zenna. I think the world and all of her."

"Well," Father Jeff declared. "We'll bring her home with us."

"Oh yes, that'd be so great. I'd love that. If things go well, I want to adopt her."

"That's good to hear, Appy. I recognize that you're getting close to her."

"Son, will she be one of the twelve?"

Appy smiled, "Certainly, of course."

Appy went back to the residence gathering room to see the tots. Zenna came over to him with her arms raised.

"Zenna missed Pap Pee."

Appy picked her up. He rocked her in his arms. He tickled her under her chin.

She giggled, "Again."

Appy asked her, "Did you wait for me to brush your teeth and put you to bed?"

Zenna giggled and said, "Watch, Zenna, dance!"

"Go for it little girl!"

He knew she was putting off going to bed.

"Zenna, when I go into town, I'm going to buy you a pair of shoes with taps on them."

"Sooes," She sleepily said.

"Yes," Appy repeated, "Shoes."

He loved listening to the toddlers learning to talk, but he always spoke correctly to them. He finally got her settled down, brushed her teeth, and put her under her blanket. He bent down on his hands and knees and played the part of animals.

"I'm a cat. I'm a sheep. I'm a cow."

The children would mimic the sounds the animals make when Appy called them off, meow, baa, and moo.

"Do bunny wabbit," Zenna asked.

"Hum, I'm not sure what a bunny rabbit does."

Zenna opened her mouth wide. She clicked her teeth loudly.

"You're right, Zenna! I've seen bunny rabbits do that with a carrot, hahahahaha. Zenna, I just can't get over your cuteness. Moreover, you're a very smart little girl."

"I smat?" Zenna asked.

"Yes…you're very smart," Appy answered. "I need to make a tape recording of every one of you tots to mail to my friend, Sister Jenny."

The children rolled over. Appy signaled Sister Myra of his departure. He turned off the lights.

CHAPTER 6

Appy woke up excited. He knew the game day would be busy. He was having coffee with Father Jeff and Father Reed while a slight morning rain was helping to make the field more playable and less bothersome for the spectators. The toddlers and young future ball players were also coming to watch the game. Rahl and Ruthy came in early. Ruthy was very friendly. Appy knew that he liked her right off. She seemed right for, Rahl. They brought Ladi and her pups with them. Appy put an old but clean and comfortable blanket in the cage for mom and her pups.

Father Jeff said to Ruthy, "I understand you have allergies to long hair animals."

"Yes, I was blessed with that. I think Rahl likes Ladi, Keena, and Biff more than me."

"I like you Ruthy just a little bit more, but just a very little bit."

Ruthy punched Rahl on the arm. She laughed. Everybody else laughed, too.

Appy announced, "It's time we get out on the field to start our work."

Ruthy said, "We'll need a couple more hands to put up this wild-ball fencing."

Father Jeff and Father Reed volunteered to hold the poles. Appy and Rahl dug the four holes and mixed the quick drying cement while the Fathers held the poles in the holes. Appy and Rahl poured the cement in and covered the top of the cement with Nairi soil. It was going to take about two hours for the cement to set, so everybody went back to the gathering room. Ladi had fed her pups. She wanted out to be with the children. The toddlers were just tall enough to allow them to pet her ears. She loved it. Everyone chatted while watching the children interact.

Appy mentioned, "Keena and Biff are getting chubby and strong looking."

"Yes," Ruthy answered. "Keena nipped at Biff the other day. He was getting too rough with her. Their teeth are becoming very sharp. They often bite on Rahl's earlobes."

Rahl laughed, "That's what happens when you let them on your shoulder. They want to cuddle in your neck. Suck blood out of your earlobes. Their sucking ability is like a magnet and those damn little teeth hurt like hell. We need to watch that they don't do a job on these toddlers."

"We need to especially watch out for, Jimi," Appy said. "He's not too keen on the pups. We can bring Ladi and her pups out on the field in their cage. Ladi won't feel so left out, and at the same time, cover the cage so that no dust gets in their eyes."

Rahl said, "Just in case, I brought dry eye drops for the pups in the event they get too much dust."

Appy answered, "That'll work."

Later in the morning, Father Reed served coffee with cake. He had asked the cooks to bake it for his guests. Moreover, everyone enjoyed it. Ruthy said, "Please compliment the cooks. I know that treat will hold me over until the cookout later in the day."

Everybody went back to the poles and found them solid in the ground. Appy and Rahl followed Ruthy's directions. Father Reed had an old ladder that he loaned them.

"I'm not sure," Father Reed mentioned, "why we had the chain links, top poles, and strips behind the shed. Maybe it was to build an enclosure for the young to play in. It was here when I came. I can see this is going to work, nicely."

Everybody was so surprised at how sturdy the fence was. It looked professionally done.

Appy informed Ruthy and Rahl, "The teens are going to be amazed."

"I have something else that's amazing, Ap."

"What's that, Rahl?"

"Come with me to the jeep."

Appy and Rahl walked back to the front of the residence where Rahl parked his jeep. There was a large box in the back of Rahl's jeep covered up.

"It's from Sister Jenny."

"Oh gosh, help me open it, Rahl."

The box was too heavy for one person to carry off the jeep. The two had a difficult time with its weight. Finally, they resorted to pushing it off.

"Who put this box in the jeep, Rahl?"

"Two strong air UPS guys."

"Gee, we're in need of weight lifting classes," Appy laughed.

"Yeah, you're right, Ap. When I look in the mirror, I only think I look like Tarzan," Rahl chuckled.

Appy took out his pocketknife. He opened the crate. There were at least twenty mitts, ten bats, several balls, and two hats that had been embroidered Coach on one, Assistant Coach on the other. Sure enough, she sent a baseball rulebook. The bats wrapped nicely with brown and white tee shirts with baseball decals on the front, were a welcome sight. Under all that, were twenty baseball-billed caps for the children adjustable at the back and five tutus for the cheerleaders that looked homemade? Appy tucked Sister Jenny's letter in his pocket. He thought that was private between him and her.

"This just makes my whole day." Appy declared.

"I imagine so, Ap."

"There'll be nothing but excitement on the field, Rahl."

"We want the young children six through eleven behind the fence with Sister Clare and the toddlers, as well. I'm sure the women who attend will help the Sister. Even though, this could prove to be a tiring day, it'll be an exciting one for every one of Sisters of Amity residents. We want them to feel like one big family playing together, eating together, and communicating with each other."

"Sarah should be coming soon. I asked her to pick up Brent, Kaela, and Lamar on her way out. I told her that all three would be waiting outside the village—just smile and say, *'Bonjour, Kaela.'* If she says, *'est-ce que vous parlez francias,'* you say, *'je ne parle pas francias.'* She'll be fine; it's only five miles from the village to Sisters of Amity."

The drive to the village proved to be pleasant for, Sarah. However, when pulling up next to the barbed wire fencing, the children of the village saddened her. She thought Appy was right when he said it might upset her as it did him and Father Jeff. Brent, Kaela, and Lamar came out with cheerful smiles. Both Kaela and Brent held Sarah's hand. Their warmth made it possible to overlook the difference in language and the environment. Sarah got out of her car. She opened the back door for Kaela and Lamar.

She pointed to the front passenger side to, Brent, "je *ne parle pas francias.*"

Lamar answered in English. "That's okay."

She shook Lamar's hand. He blushed. When she went to start the car, it sputtered—not wanting to turn over. Brent got out, pulled up the hood, and cleaned the filter. To Sarah's surprise, the car started right up. It sounded as normal as always. Sarah clapped her hands to acknowledge her appreciation that Brent was there. That he also knew something about cars. Who'd have guessed? After that, they were taking the road without incident.

Sarah pulled up behind Rahl's jeep.

Appy opened the car doors and shook Brent's hand while acknowledging Kaela and Lamar.

He reached out for Sarah's hand, and walked with her into the gathering room. The rest followed.

Sarah made the comment, "It's good to be here. The hospital was a zoo this morning. There was a school bus crash and each child had to be thoroughly examined, some x-rays, some stitches, so fortunate for everybody that nobody was seriously hurt. I'll take those bruises and cuts anytime given the alternatives."

"For sure," Appy responded. "Sarah, you know Father Jeff and Father Reed."

"Well, we know her as, Dr. Sarah," said Father Jeff. "However, it's even better, more personal, to know her as, Sarah."

"Thank you," Sarah replied.

Appy thought to himself, "*Leave it to Father Jeff to say all the right things.*" "Sarah, you met Kaela, but would you like to say something to her now that I can interpret for you?"

"Yes, ask her if my driving made her nervous?"

"No, not at all, whatever gave her that idea?" Kaela asked.

"Good, I usually travel somewhat slowly and most of my passengers notice that. I see a lot in the emergency room, so I'm a cautious driver."

"*Excusez-moi, s'il vous plait*, Kaela. Sarah…I want you to meet, Ruthy."

He put his hand at the small of her back guiding her toward Rahl and Ruthy. He introduced Sarah and Ruthy. The four chatted.

Appy asked Ruthy, "Do you think you could make me an adorable hat like Rahl's?"

Everybody broke out in laughter.

"I'm serious."

"If only you knew how he teased me about my hat, Ruthy," Rahl chuckled, "you should answer with a big fat no."

"Rahl, you're a traitor. I had no idea how obnoxious, bothersome, and stinging these little, black-winged insects were here in Nairi. Ruthy, I take it all back."

"I'll forgive you this time, Ap. Yes, of course, I'll stitch you up a netting hat." Ruthy said with a smile.

Father Reed asked the new guests if they wanted to finish off the cake with coffee. All agreed, since it'd be a while before the game was over and food served again.

Father Reed motioned, "Come this way to the kitchen. I'll set you up. We have large tables to seat everyone."

The tables were made of four 4x8-plywood sheets with sawhorses to hold them up. It worked well with so many children. The Sisters made nice pads and tablecloths to cover them before their sewing machine quit. Nothing could pass for a display in a home improvement magazine, that's for sure, but it worked for the simple needs of the children and clergy in this home.

Appy conversed with his friends about his plans of bringing all the children together in play.

"The young ones will be told that they'll be the players in future games. It'll do them good to watch the older players to see how the game goes. At the end of the game, the teens will put the younger players up to bat and run bases giving them a taste of what's to come. It should be amusing to watch. If we feel a need to laugh, we should turn our heads. What we don't need is tears of disappointment. The coach is very sensitive to the feelings of his players."

Everyone did a thumb up. Appy related everything said—to Brent, Kaela, and Lamar. He then asked everyone to come outside to watch while he and Rahl played a little ball with Lamar. Appy knew that umpiring would be different, but Lamar would learn that in time.

"Rahl, let's throw the ball back and forth for now."

"Okay, I can do that," Rahl answered.

For a while, the ball just wouldn't go into Lamar's mitt, repeatedly they put the ball in motion. After twenty or more tries of grabbing at the ball from midair, suddenly Lemar caught on. Appy knew he was smart and agile too. Nothing meant more to Appy than putting these children in team play. He knew Lamar might be the only hope for inspiring the village children to play ball. As umpire, he'd learn every aspect of baseball. Lamar, of course, would need to learn English—at least the English that pertained to baseball. He had already picked up some English, which came about easily. His parents would also benefit in time.

"Lamar how did the children like the apples?" Appy, asked loudly.

Lamar hollered back, "They all know who Appy is now. An apple is like a Christmas gift."

"Lamar is your village mostly Catholic?"

"Yes, they're mostly Catholic, but not all." Lamar answered.

Appy thought he'd relate that to Father Jeff.

Kaela and Brent enjoyed the French conversation that Appy and Lamar were having. They seemed proud of their boy. Happy for him since this was a thrilling moment in his life.

Brent was hollering, "Catch that ball."

Lamar would respond, "Pipe down, Dad."

Appy thought that Brent was probably typical of most fathers. He wasn't sure not having had that experience, but it made sense. It turned three o'clock—Sister Clare and the teens escorted the young players to their mats behind the fence.

Sister Clare later told Appy, "You should have been there to see the teens and how excited they were about the fence. The teens were also very friendly and kind to the younger players."

"That's great, Sister."

At the gathering room, Sister Myra and Sadie were getting the toddlers ready. The cooks were going to care for the babies since they didn't have to make dinner.

"Sarah, this is Zenna," Appy whispered. "All children are special, but she's very special to me. Will you take care of her?"

"She's adorable, Ap. I'll take good care of her." Sarah answered.

Zenna danced around Appy. The two curly ponytails on top of her head bounced with her every movements. Sarah took Zenna's hand. She followed the rest at the end of the line. Sister Myra led Ukita,

Tobi, Jimi, Aarif, Uni, Sarah, and Zenna out to the field. Luckily, the children didn't recognize Sarah as the doctor that pricked them, but than again, the nurses did that job.

When everybody was on the field and water jugs placed, the team gathered around, Appy.

Gbandi said, "We really like the fence, Ap. It's an exciting day."

"Well, that's great. Let me start the play." Appy announced, "First team up, call it heads or tails?"

Team 2 was to be first up to bat. Sadie sang the National Anthem. The cheerleaders put their tutus over their shorts and baseball tee shirts over the tops they were wearing. Appy passed out mitts, baseball billed caps, and shirts to the rest of the team. The teens looked like they were about to explode with energy and excitement.

Appy said, "If you give me that much enthusiasm on the field, I'll be so happy."

It looked like the tee shirts would be a little bit big for the younger ones, but fine for the teens. Team 2 was behind the fence, lined up, and ready. The outfielders and basemen of team 1 were standing in their positions. It was going to be different today. More difficult for the teens because all balls would be in flight rather than on the ground. Appy and Rahl warmed the players up by throwing the ball back and forth—to get players acquainted with mitt catches.

Finally, Appy hollered, "Batter up!"

The game was exciting for everyone. Sadie started everybody off with tears due to the beauty in her voice. The cheerleaders rooted for both teams. Appy would stop by to check on Sarah and Zenna between innings.

"I can see why you find her so…darling. She sits by me saying, 'Ball one, styke two.' If I root, she roots. The game is so much fun to watch. The younger players are watching intently knowing their fun is coming up."

Appy replied smiling, "I noticed that."

Sister Myra loved her hat. She enjoyed lining up the team for play.

Appy gave Sarah his cap, "Will you be my, girl?"

Sarah's cheeks turned pink as she replied, "Certainly, do you think I'd miss out on all this fun?"

Appy did a thumbs up, "Yes, I won't disappoint you, girl."

The two seemed to mesh from the very start. This day absolutely proved their attraction to each other.

Jayla called the game. Her scorecard said five runs for team one, four runs for team two. The runs were much less with the ball in flight, but the two teams were equally as good in action. The older teens took the younger future players out on the field letting them bat and catch balls.

Appy requested of the girls, "Please help Sister Myra with the toddlers. Don't let them beyond the fence while the younger ones are practicing. Rahl, Brent, and I are going to start a fire in the pit, put the grill on top, and cook us up some dogs."

They took the dogs off the grill, placed them in buns, and kept them heated in the wrappers until serving time. The three men cooked hot dogs until there were no more buyers. Sarah had brought a big bag of lollipops and bubble gum for the players.

"That was a good plan, Sarah," Appy said smiling. "We all chewed while keeping our mouths shut to avoid the dust."

The toddlers surely enjoyed sucking the yummy juices that lingered from the lollipops. Of course, the Sisters watched the little ones closely. The toddlers enjoyed the taste of everything. Ladi enjoyed the falling crumbs and licking faces.

After eating, everyone's face needed washing. The toddlers were walked back to the resident home around seven o'clock in the evening and Sister Myra set-up the children's pillow bedding. She tucked them in. They were off to sleep in no time, absolutely exhausted by a day of activity unknown to their little moving spirits. All the young players and teens were tired out, too. A quiet rest seems needed to wind down this exciting day's activity.

Gbandi told Appy, "It was the best time I've had in my whole life."

"Gbandi, this is my girl, Sarah. Gbandi is going to be my apprentice, Sarah."

"It's good that you'll be working with a very knowledgeable person. Take advantage of this great opportunity. I must say, Gbandi, I enjoyed watching you in play—great out fielding."

"Thank you," Gbandi replied with proudness in his smile.

Appy made mention, "After school tomorrow, Gbandi, you and Chikae can come to the shed outback to work with me."

"Okay, but right now I'm going back to digest the four dogs I just ate and rest up."

"All right—see you tomorrow after school."

"Ap—Ruthy and I should be getting back to the mission house with Ladi and the pups before the wind kicks up, setting my jeep on top of some mountain."

"Oh Rahl," Ruthy said laughing. "You say the funniest things."

"Hey, Ap," Rahl said. "We could take Kaela, Brent and Lamar back with us if Sarah wants to stay longer."

"Sure," Sarah answered. "However, my stay won't be much longer if I want some daylight to travel by."

Father Jeff and Father Reed picked up all the mitts and bats. Rahl brought them back to the shed in his jeep. The two priests were so happy with the wonderful day. The pleasure everyone enjoyed.

Sarah and Appy found themselves deserted by everyone. Either everyone was tired from the long day and heat, or they were giving the couple a little time to get to know each other better. The two walked back to the shed to get a little time alone.

"This isn't the best place to entertain you, Sarah, but all the other rooms here are busy. Have a seat."

"When do you think you'll be coming to the hospital next, Ap?"

"In about two days, I'll have the computers ready that need to go back there. I need to stay there until everything is connected and running well. Mr. Cronc mentioned that the emergency room should definitely have two of them soon. Do you think that maybe we could have lunch together?"

"Well, you'll have to e-mail me the day before. I'll see if I can meet with you and Rahl."

"Sarah, I'm trying to get that car in back of this shed in running condition. When I have it operating, I'd like to take you out to a nice place to eat, something that resembles a real date."

"Oh, I really enjoyed today. It's what I think a perfect date is. I thought you were so handsome and a picture of unity on the field. Ap, you must know that I love children as much as you do by the career I've chosen. Today you showed me what you are made of."

"What's that, Sarah—sugar and spice and everything nice?"

"You're being silly, Ap. I'm serious. I see a person who loves for all the right reasons."

"Oh, most especially, for what I feel is right about you, girl."

He kissed her softly. She felt safe in his arms enjoying the sweetness of his lips.

"Sarah, I know you're the one for me, so sweet and beautiful—my dream."

"Thank you, Ap; those are the loveliest words I've ever heard."

Sarah thought that the two should talk a little more to get to know each other better.

"Zenna is so cute, Ap. Would you like a little girl like that when you marry?"

"I want many girls and boys from little babies to teens. I am seriously thinking of adopting Zenna once I am back in the states. We'll be taking her back with us. Father Jeff will help me out in the adoption process. Sarah, what do you think of Gbandi? I think it's a shame."

Sarah nodded, "I wonder what'll happen when he turns eighteen and has to go off on his own to make a life for himself."

"I know, Sarah, it just eats at me because I know what a boy like that wants most: His own people."

The conversation continued with ease. Appy was feeling very relaxed around her.

"Sarah, we better get you on your way back before darkness sets in. I hate to see you drive out of here alone at night."

He walked her to her car that looked a different color in the dusk that was setting in. He pushed her hair back gently and kissed her good-bye very lovingly.

"Sarah, that kiss has to last me way too long. E-mail me every night because I never know when you're not on duty."

"I'll try to get some kind of schedule for you, Ap. Of course, I never know about emergency situations."

"Sure, I understand that. All I ask is that you don't wear anybody else's baseball cap."

"I promise you, I'll never do that, Ap." Sarah said with a wink and a smile.

Sarah rolled up her window. She headed home. Appy thought to himself, *"What a truly awe-inspiring day this was with all my friends, the Sisters, the Fathers, and children of all ages."* Most importantly a day in which he connected with Sarah's inner being.

Appy went to his room and wrote, Sister Jenny.

Dear Sister Jenny,

How can I ever thank you enough? I could have written you on Father Jeff's e-mail, but I thought it more personal in my own hand. If I missed one person this day of our first baseball game, it was you. I was so thrilled that all the equipment, baseball clothing, and caps came today, the day of the big game. Can you just imagine how excited the children and I were? Sister Myra loved her cap. She wore it through the whole game. She wants to write to thank you herself. For everyone who assisted you in this magnificent and charitable endeavor, I'm sending a "thank you note" to put on the board in the vestibule of the church.

Sister Jenny, as to the personal side of my life, I've met a girl here. Her name is Sarah Henderson. She's an intern in pediatrics here in Africa. She's beautiful to my eye—as sweet as you are. How strange that I had to come all the way around the world to find someone to fall in love with. I believe that you'll just love her. Please pray that everything will turn out well for the two of us because I'm crazy about her.

I'm tired after this rousing game day, so I'll close for now. Say hello to Sister Eunice, Father Larry, and everyone else at St. Matthew. I'll write you on e-mail next. Father Jeff was so excited to be able to connect with St. Matthew. I bet you were happy, as well. I hear you have another box of equipment you're sending me. The more the better, but by now you must be tiring at the thought of shipping air parcels.

Forever, Appy

P.S. They call me "Ap" here. What do you think of that?

While Appy was getting ready for bed, he saw the letter from Sister Jenny sticking slightly out of his pocket. He had forgotten the letter altogether. He took it out to read it.

Hello Appy,

It's good to hear that Father Jeff and you are well and adjusting to the hot climate in Africa. We miss you both. Sister Eunice and Father Larry say hello—that they'll write soon. I'll bet the children at the African home enjoy you. Our babies miss you feeding them. I'm going to send some film. Will you please take some pictures to help keep us involved in your journey? I'm, of course, interested in seeing the children on the field wearing their shirts, caps, and enjoying all their equipment.

The people of St. Matthew's church are so good about doing the right thing. They came through with such grace.

Darkness was setting in, a time for Appy to wind down, and enable him to reflect upon tomorrow's baseball schedule, envision the young players teaming up, while expecting the teens to stand behind them rooting at every turn. Most of all, coaching in a friendly, enjoyable manner while hoping that everyone will find fun in the game of baseball. He went back to the shed. Sarah had e-mailed that she returned home safely.

Back in his room, he put on his pajamas and went to check on Zenna and the others. She was asleep, next to a little friend with a blanket pulled up close to her face, looking very sweet, tempting Appy to kiss her chubby, little cheeks. However, not wanting to wake anyone, and possibly undo the peace and quiet Sister Myra was enjoying, he returned to his room and went to bed.

CHAPTER 7

The next morning Appy, Father Jeff, and Father Reed were having breakfast when Zenna came in the kitchen looking for Appy. She went up to him and sat on his lap.

"How are you this morning, Sweetheart?"

"I fine."

Appy looked at Father Jeff, "We need to do all we can to secure this relationship between Zenna and me."

"I'll do everything in my power to help you out, Ap. Of course, your status will have a lot to do with it—like having a stable job, marital status, and a home that's safe for children. I'm sure Father Reed and I will give you great character references. We still have a couple years here, so you need to care for her like a father. The first five years of a child's life is a most important bonding experience."

"Yes, who knows, I may ask Sarah to marry me—look to Rahl's father for a job; and search for a big old home or farm where the children could play baseball, skate, and run their dogs."

"Sounds wonderful," Father Reed said. "I wish you the best of luck in all your future endeavors. I know you'll make the greatest father to her!"

"Thank you." Appy replied.

The morning shower was definitely preparing the field for the young children to begin their training period, but no real game seemed playable until Appy could see a certain amount of confidence building in the young players. Since he had time before the children got out of school, he thought he'd wash that old car out back. Lo and behold, after clearing the dust off the metal surface, the car didn't look so old after all. He looked at the mileage gage—it read 98,000, which wasn't too bad in his estimation. He was going to e-mail an auto dealership to order the part he felt to be the problem source. In the meantime, Father Reed had given him the keys to the car, so he thought that after he cleaned the exterior, the interior, all oil and air engine filters, he'd attempt to start it in the event he was off on his diagnosis. Father Jeff came out to watch Appy at work.

"Appy, that car looks good, no rust or dents. The tires look decent, too."

"Yes, well there's no ice, snow, or salt to eat at it. That probably has a lot to do with it. I'm quite sure?"

"Most certainly," Father Jeff said, "a car's frame must last forever in Africa."

"Here goes—say a prayer, Father. I've cleaned everything under the hood and now I'm ready to give it a try."

Putting the key in the ignition, turning it, hearing some sputtering sounds, the engine turned over.

"You have the best luck, Appy."

"Wow, I can't believe it. If I can get this car to town, I'll have the wires and hoses under the hood checked out. Hop in, Father. We should drive around to the front entrance, so Father Reed can see it."

Father Reed heard a horn. He went out front to investigate a sound he seldom ever heard at the home.

"For goodness sake, Appy," Father Reed said enthusiastically, "you just constantly astound me. In my estimation, that vehicle was put out to pasture never to operate again. Consider it your car Appy for the rest of your stay here in Nairi."

"Thanks Father Reed, but you and Father Jeff can also enjoy trips to town while I stay here to help with the children."

"Yes," answered Father Jeff. "We could enjoy having lunch at a nice restaurant or shopping for food we like without calling that old, dust covered taxi that rattles all the way to town."

"I'll e-mail, Rahl. Ask him to bring some gas tomorrow. I know he keeps 25-gallon cans for his jeep at the mission house. I've no idea how much gas is in this little red sedan. I wonder if it'll even operate the whole way. I believe Father Reed—you said it'd just take a notion to quit running."

"Yes," Father Reed answered.

"Well then, I better have Rahl follow me into town."

Father Jeff got out of the car, and walked to the entrance with Father Reed. Appy drove the car around back and parked it next to the shed. He went into the shed to check his messages. He thought to himself that the color display on the desktops was magnificent and rewarding.

Rahl had e-mailed, Ap,

> Hi Ap,
>
> I'm coming out today to help you in training the young players. I'm bringing Ruthy and the dogs because she so enjoyed watching the children at the last game. She's bringing finger sandwiches for the players, enough for everyone, topping it off with brownies as a treat. We'll pick up Lamar for the workout. I already e-mailed his father. Rahl

Appy e-mailed back,

> Rahl that's great! Would you bring me some gas—just enough to get into town tomorrow? I

managed to start that car out back. Can you believe that? See you soon—that girl of your's rocks. Ap

Appy went in and informed the cooks that Ruthy was bringing snack food for the children. Zenna came running. Appy picked her up. He asked her if she wanted to take a walk to see his car.

He took her hand. "C'mon little girl," the two walked to the shed. She saw the car, "wed car."

"Yes, a red car. I talked to Rahl today, Zenna; and he said he's bringing Ladi and her pups to see us. Do you like the puppies, dear?"

"Yep, when no be bad—pease, welcome, tank you."

Appy thought, *"It's as if she's saying, 'I'm polite. You may choose the term that fits the situation best.'"* "You're so funny, Zenna!" Appy laughed.

"Yep, I funny," she giggled.

"I'm thinking, Zenna, of getting you a puppy all your own. Of the pups, honey, which one is your favorite, Keena or Biff?"

"I ike Beef." Zenna said giggling.

It crossed Appy's mind that she was smart enough to pick up the word "bad" because Jimi showed fear when the puppy was sucking on his toe. Ironically, it seemed to be a behavior learned from her little friend. He sat down beside her on the bench next to the shed. He began to explain to her that puppies could be warm, protective and loving—just like, Ladi. He also let her know how happy she could be with her own doggie.

"Zenna, be happy with puppy."

"Yes, Zenna will be happy with her own puppy," Appy answered.

"I'm happy with Pap Pee, too."

"Oh, Zenna, you're a little cutie!"

He kissed her on her forehead, which was one of the loving and meaningful gestures that Appy had internalized from his childhood; clearly demonstrating that Sister Jenny had so much influence on him during his growing years.

Appy sat Zenna on his stool in the shed. She watched a cartoon while he worked on computers. He laid out parts and containers for Gbandi and Chikae to commit to memory. He also laid out an open computer with all its components exposed in an effort to entice their curiosity. He whistled all the while that he worked. Zenna seemed very content to be in Appy's shed. He could hear her trying to repeat words off the computer, and could see her pucker up her lips to whistle like him. "Well, little girl, it's about time we go have some lunch."

"Okeydokey, I eat with Pap Pee," Zenna, said.

Appy took hold of her hand. They swung their arms in midair as Zenna sang the words she heard on the computer. Lunch was very good. Zenna took her nap without complaint. Appy found it amazing how a little unexpected activity caused these toddlers to tire out easily, but than again, their brains work very hard every day for learning purposes.

Appy began to think about the training game. He piled up the bases, bats, and mitts in the car. He brought them to the field wishing to eliminate the job Rahl was always stuck with. There hadn't been any rainfall this morning. Nevertheless, the wind was somewhere up in the clouds and not touching ground—giving Appy the impression that the heavens were with him again today. He drove back to the home. Rahl and Ruthy were just pulling in. Rahl stopped the car and leaped out. He and Lamar rushed to see Appy's auto.

"You're a winner, Ap," Rahl said.

Ruthy went inside to give the cooks the little sandwiches. She stopped to have a nice conversation with Father Jeff.

"Ruthy dear, my mouth has been watering to taste that roast beef and potato combination dish you make."

"Oh—did Rahl tell you that he liked that meal?"

"Yes, he said you'd have us over sometime to enjoy it."

"He didn't mention that to me, but I'd love to have you—Father Reed, Sarah, and Ap for dinner. I will see to it, soon."

"That'd be great because my mother always made that dish." He winked at her.

In the meantime, Rahl and Appy unlatched the cap of the car's gas tank, and poured the gas in.

"I hope this car makes it into town, Rahl. It seemed as if the filters clogged up the engine so badly it wouldn't turn over. I'll pull it into the gas station in town to see what's up with it. I talked with Sarah last night. She's getting excited to see us tomorrow. Too bad, she couldn't make it here today, but she has teaching rounds."

The field began to be flooded with children and teens. The teens were putting shirts on the young players. Though a bit too big, they'd work just fine. They were explaining to the teams that every batter had to wear a helmet. Helmets were scarce and needed badly—having only two helmets and umpire protection. Appy was giving much thought about helmets today, but because the children were in training, he felt that the throws wouldn't be that powerful. The teens needed to watch for balls going too fast or in the wrong direction. Gbandi was doing a terrific teaching job at organizing the players and outfielders, but seeing how far out they were—Appy hollered out,

"Gbandi, bring the outfielders in some."

Sadie—who Appy called "little mother" was lining up the players. She also was instructing on drinking water. She was doing all she could to help Sister Myra.

Appy certainly appreciated her genuine goodness. He whispered in her ear, "Sadie, you're the best."

"Thank you, Ap. I want to be of help."

"You bet girl. You're always a big help."

"Are we ready guys and gals? Sadie tells me that Ajani is first up to bat—then Tanesha, Zalika, and Jabarl. She'll continue to call off the rest of the names to you."

Just then, Father Jeff came out on the field carrying Zenna. Appy walked up to him and held her.

"Zenna woke up. She wanted you, so I thought I'd bring her out to see the game."

Appy knew Father Jeff was warming up to Zenna because he felt she'd be in his future life. To Appy, it looked like Zenna with her grandpa.

"Wow," Appy thought. "*What a sign of his devotion to me.*"

Father Jeff put his arms out for her.

"You go with Father Jeff and watch the game," Appy said to her.

"Pay styke two?"

"Yes, you be a good little girl and watch."

"Ajani," Appy said loudly. "You're up."

Rahl was in outfield with Gbandi. Ajani got up to bat. He was a handsome looking little fellow seeming to be very competitive with a habit of spitting out wads of dust—looking to kill the ball if he could.

Sure enough, he hit the ball, ran to first base, ran to second base, and made a short cut across the pitcher plate for home.

"Ajani!" Appy said startled, "you need to run three bases and then home."

"No! This way is easier and faster. I'm not running that way."

Lamar looked at Appy because it crossed his mind, *"How do I call this?"*

"You're OUT!" Appy shouted.

Lamar repeated, "You're OUT!"

Ajani began to pout, threw his arms up in the air, and wobbled in anger to the bench.

Rahl said to Gbandi in outfield, "Ajani looks pissed."

"Ajani," Appy said quietly, "baseball has rules that must be followed."

Off to the side, Appy asked Sister Myra, "How old is Ajani?"

"He's six." She answered.

"Oh gosh, he's so young and cute. He definitely wants to be a winner! It's hard to keep a straight face."

The teens were now feeling responsible for the success of the younger team. All seemed to work so hard at making the young ones understand the game. Appy could see Gbandi slapping the hand of a young outfielder when she was successful in the catch and throw back of balls—a clear sign of leadership, and a characteristic that Appy found admirable.

Zenna sat on Father Jeff's lap the whole time hollering out, "Ball one, styke two, home won,"

Father Jeff laughingly said to Appy, "I was getting confused with the real plays on the field—not knowing who was funnier Zenna or the young players."

Appy was trying so hard to keep his composure. Father Jeff wasn't helping. Appy backed away with his hand cupped over his mouth.

It was time to stop for the day. A time to enjoy the good sandwiches, brownies, and quench their thirst with some flavored drinks and needed rest. Appy said, "Everyone played very well today. The day after tomorrow you'll do even better. I think those brownies were awesome, how about you?"

The young ones and teens answered, "Great!" Ruthy could hear the musical clapping that the children made. Appy cheerfully said, "See everyone the day after tomorrow."

Ajani ran up to Sister Clare, "I liked those little sandwiches. They tasted good."

The practice was over. The young players went to the living quarters that housed their age group. Ruthy, Rahl, and Lamar put Ladi and her pups in the jeep to head back to the mission house.

Ruthy's whole demeanor was one of excitement and happiness because she knew her finger sandwiches and dessert went over big with the children and adults, as well. Appy shook the hand of Lamar and Rahl.

Rahl said to Appy, "See you tomorrow, sport."

Gbandi came to the shed after the practice. When Appy saw him, the two began to laugh uncontrollably.

"Oh dear," Appy said, "Lamar was really confused as to how to call Ajani's run."

Appy put his hands on Gbandi's shoulders. He ripped into a roaring laughter again.

"It was so cute," Gbandi said. "When Tanesha would hit the ball, and do a complete turn around every time. Of course, Jabarl looked a bit strange—as if cutting a piece of cake, the way he chopped down on the ball."

"I know, Gbandi," Appy chuckled. "Everyone will be laughing in their sleep tonight. I know I've laughed myself out, so I hope to sleep well."

"Me too," Gbandi answered. "I've a headache from laughing so hard."

Gbandi was finding the shed with its electronic equipment interesting and listened carefully to everything Appy was teaching. Chikae wasn't feeling well this day. He slept in even while the practice was going on. Sister Clare thought it was a touch of the flu. Others would probably come down soon. She hoped it might pass by the staff and Sisters since it would be hard on everyone else to get through the worst of it without them.

CHAPTER 8

Sure enough, early the next day, Rahl e-mailed Appy that he had come down with the flu. Telling Appy to drive to the mission and take his jeep into town. Appy replied that he'd take Gbandi and Lamar with him to town since it was Saturday and school is out. He thought this excursion could only be good for the two of them. Appy felt that Lamar must feel a little left out due to the language difference. That Gbandi could help Lamar with his English while building a rapport with him that both could enjoy. Appy thought he'd see how the car performed while driving to the village, then on to the mission house before attempting the drive to town. All the while, hoping the car would make it into town, so he could have it looked at. He guessed that the boys could endure a five-mile walk for help in the event the car gave out. He'd bring water to clean filters, also for drinking, along with some apples for energy.

Gbandi and Appy took off around nine o'clock in the morning to pick up, Lamar.

"Pray Gbandi, this car may not make it. We may have to walk to the village swamped by flies, wishing we hadn't trusted this vehicle."

"Oh, do we have to talk about it," Gbandi answered.

To Appy's wonderment, the car did fine the whole way to the village. Once again, Brent and Appy cleaned the filters well. While setting everything back in place, Brent told Appy about Sarah's car clogging up the same way.

"Are you kidding me? She never said one word about that to me. What do you think, Brent, will we make it to the mission house?"

"Yes, I think so. If the car gets sluggish, keep cleaning the filters."

Lamar jumped in the back seat. Naturally, the conversation went to the young player's practice.

Lamar laughingly stated, "It was so funny when Zalika ran to first base carrying the bat all the way. I turned to avoid losing it because I had already witnessed Ajani's strange run along with a few other confusing plays that made it very hard to suppress my laughing mechanism."

Appy said, "Nobody was looking at anybody for fear of falling apart."

The three had another good laugh.

Lamar commented, "My, dad and I, laughed all the way through dinner until my mother said, "Okay that's enough you two."

The two boys were having fun exchanging words from their respective languages while enlisting Appy's help, *bon*-good, *demain*-tomorrow, *manger*-to eat, *maison*-home, *balle*-ball, *je suis* Lamar (I am Lamar). The boys continued until they reached the mission house.

"Hey," Gbandi said. "We're here with no problems."

"Yeah," Appy answered, "You pray well, Gbandi."

Ruthy came outside so as not to expose anyone and said Rahl had a bad night, but was sleeping very sound now. She gave the boys some cookies. She also handed them some money equivalent to ten dollars American money telling them to spend it on their venture. She handed Appy her wireless computer.

"E-mail me in the event the car breaks down. I'll be happy to pick you guys up if you run into trouble."

"Oh thanks, Ruthy," Appy said. "I must say the boys didn't necessarily like the idea of a five-mile hike."

"No, I suppose not," she chuckled. "Good thing you fixed this wireless computer."

"Nevertheless, Ruthy, the boys will enjoy spending the money very much. Did you fellows say 'thank you' to Ruthy?"

"The boys said 'thank you' with their smiles," Ruthy chuckled again.

"Yeah," Gbandi said.

On the road, Appy told the boys that he had much to do when getting into town.

"First, we'll go to the gas station and have the mechanic look over the car. Maybe the attendants will give us a loaner for the day. Then you need to wait patiently while I install the emergency room's computers at the hospital. Afterwards, lunch with Sarah should be to your liking. When lunch is over, we'll bring her back. The rest of the day, we can shop. I need to get Zenna some patent leather shoes that I promised her, also a tape recorder to tape the children's voices to send to my dear friend Sister Jenny at St. Matthew. After doing all that, should we feel up to it, we can stop at the sporting goods store to see if they have some outdated helmets that I can buy cheap."

Pulling into the station, Appy began talking to the master mechanic about the problem he and Father Reed had experienced with the car. Appy asked the mechanic if he had a car to loan him on this busy day he had planned.

The owner said, "Yes, you can take my truck. It's a piece of junk, but it runs good."

Apply replied, "As long as it runs good, that's all that counts."

Their next stop was at the hospital where the doctors in the emergency room were thrilled to get their computers back in working condition. While there, Appy had a long conversation with two of the doctors—Dr. Sodi and Dr. Reese who asked him if he did repairs on the side.

"Well, I have two boys that I am training who'd love to do some repair work for a little money. The boys live at Sisters of Amity and need all the help they can muster to develop skills that are in demand today. Of course, I'll do the final inspection on the machines, and back the work. I come this way every other week. If you e-mail me, I'll come to the emergency room area to pick them up."

Appy shook hands with Dr. Sodi and Dr. Reese, "I'm hoping to take my doctor gal out for lunch today."

"Who's that?" Dr. Sodi asked.

"Sarah Henderson, she's in pediatric training here." Appy answered.

"Oh," Dr. Sodi said, "Dr. Reese and I know her well. She's a beautiful woman and an excellent intern. If I weren't married, I'd probably make a pass at that chick myself."

"She's my cup of tea for sure, so hands off." Appy chuckled.

Appy went to the waiting room to get the boys after he had picked up his paycheck from human resources.

He informed the boys, "We have time to spare, so we can drive around town to see where everything is. That's a nice restaurant over there, a good eating-place to take Sarah on a real date tomorrow night. Can anyone spot where the movie house is?"

Gbandi pointed and said, "Its right over there on the left side of the street."

"Oh yes, let's park here to see what's playing. We can walk down the street a ways to see what stores they have on the main street." Appy thought the town was somewhat sophisticated considering what the average African in the outer communities suffered.

They spotted an old store. The three went inside to look around. Gbandi and Lamar bought a faux leather wallet to hold their paper money. Appy tried to give them a little more money, but Lamar said, "Oh, my dad gave me some extra money to shop with—give it to Gbandi."

"Okay, I hope you guys find something you really want."

Gbandi said, "I know I want a pair of jeans or cargo pants with pockets on both sides and maybe a candy bar. It's been a long time since I had a candy bar."

Appy replied, "I think you'll have enough for that. If not, I'll advance you a little, Gbandi."

Gbandi tried on a nice pair of khaki-colored cargo pants. Appy and Lamar thought they looked good, but felt jeans would be a better choice with the dust and all. Gbandi agreed. He tried on a pair of black jeans—perfect all thought. Lamar spotted a tee shirt that had black and silver stars on the front. He thought it nice for the climate in Nairi. He also liked the design very much.

"Okay guys," Appy said. "Pay for those items, we need to go pick up, Sarah."

Strange as it might seem to the average intact family unit that children would want to buy their own clothes, not Ipods and such, it wasn't strange to Appy. At times, while working in his teens, he had to meet his own necessities.

Appy drove around to the back of the hospital. Sarah came out in her blue, medical v-neck top and blue pants with drawstring ties at the front. Appy jumped out of the truck—looked at her adoringly and kissed her. He whispered in her ear how much he missed her.

"Do you have some place special where you'd like to eat lunch, Sarah?"

"There's a nice French bistro in town where I'm sure Gbandi and Lamar might get a hamburger, fries, and a cold drink. Where Lamar will also be able to order in French," Sarah answered.

"Sarah, we better drive there in your car because the gas station loaned me a three-seat-truck that won't accommodate the four of us."

"Sure, I'll drive."

Appy nudged up to Sarah speaking quietly, "Do you think we can go out to eat tomorrow night and to a movie?"

"Well, I could always pick you up if your car isn't ready."

"Oh no," Appy said. "Brent told me about your car clogging up. You know, I would have been a nervous wreck had I known that."

"Exactly, that's why I never mentioned it."

Appy strongly said, "I'll pick you up, or we stay home brave lady."

"Okay Ap, if you insist, we can do it your way."

The two held hands. Everyone walked to Sarah's car.

The boys and Appy filled Sarah in on the young player's practice. Sarah could not help but laugh. She thought how cute they probably were. How innocent about the game of baseball—most especially, the rules of the game.

Lamar spoke in French, "*monsieur*! L*e menu, s'il vous plait.*"

"Ditto," Gbandi said.

Sarah and Appy chuckled. The boys ordered burgers, fries and a cold drink. Appy had a glass of wine with a grilled chicken salad. Sarah ordered the same with coffee to drink since she was still on duty.

Sarah commented, "Ap, I think you should have another teen game. You know how we all enjoyed that—grilled hot dogs and all."

"Yes, we might do that. I just don't want to put the young players on display until they look half-way like they know the game."

Gbandi and Lamar thought that was a terrific idea Sarah had. The two cheered it on.

When it was time to get Sarah back, Lamar said to the server, "*merci mademoiselle, au revoir*!"

Sarah mentioned to Lamar, "You made us look good." Appy interpreted what Sarah said.

Lamar smiled, *Merci,* Sarah."

The boys opened Sarah's car door. The two went and stayed in the truck until Appy walked Sarah to the hospital's rear entrance door.

"Sarah, it's so hard to date when we've nowhere to go to be somewhat alone. You live in apartment housing for interns on a hospital campus. I live in a house with priests, nuns, and children. Gosh, Sarah that isn't so romantic. I suggest we find a restaurant where we're closed off from others."

"Okay Ap, the search is on."

Appy let her know he'd see her tomorrow at dinner hour.

"I'll steal a quick kiss to hold me over since I wouldn't want your colleagues teasing you for the rest of the day."

"Quite so," Sarah answered.

After dropping Sarah off, Appy and the boys went into a shoe store. Appy gave the store clerk a drawing of Zenna's foot. He also brought an old pair of shoes that Zenna could no longer wear. He informed the store clerk that she was just three years of age. The woman clerk brought out a pair of shiny patent leather shoes that Appy had requested.

He asked the clerk "Is it possible to put taps on these shoes?"

"Oh," she said in a startled manner. "You can't mean that because a three-year-old could drive you crazy with the sound."

"Is that right? I'm new at these things and learning as I go."

"Oh yes," the sales clerk said. "I've three girls in tap dance classes. They don't tap in those shoes in my house. This particular pair of shoes has a little heel on them. She'll be able to make a little noise with them."

"Okay, wrap me up two pair," Appy answered.

Hitting other stores, Appy picked up a battery-operated tape recorder with extra batteries and tapes. From the sporting goods shop, in trade for repair of the owner's slow operating computer, Appy was able to get two new helmets that were window displays. Although somewhat faded in color, it was a needed break on this expensive day. The boys bought their candy bars. In addition, a couple bags of candy pieces.

"Well boys, are we all set to go see if the car is ready?"

"Okay," Gbandi said.

Appy pulled into the station, parked the owner's truck, and went in to talk to the master mechanic who informed him that it was a short underneath the computer bank. That he also put a new-type filter that could only help keep the heavy Nairi dust away from start-up connections. The mechanic said they were lucky to have gotten this far with the problem the car had.

"Gbandi," Appy remarked. "I need to memorize your prayers."

"Sure do," Gbandi answered.

After unloading the hospital computers that needed repair, along with the one computer from the sporting goods store from the truck to the car, the three were on their way home. At the edge of town, once again, Appy pulled over at the fruit hut. He bought two-bushel baskets of apples and two-bushel baskets of oranges. The next stop was at the mission house to return Ruthy's computer. Ruthy was glad to hear that the car was fixed. She said that a UPS truck dropped off a box for him. The boys didn't think it would fit in the trunk.

So Appy said, "Put two bushel baskets of the fruit in the front with me. Let's see if the box will fit in the trunk now. I think so."

It took all three to lift it up, drop it in the trunk, and step back while the car bounced from the weight. Ruthy found some rope. While tying the trunk down, Appy asked, "How's Rahl doing?"

"A little better, he ate some toast dunked in coffee."

"It'll probably take a couple more days." Appy replied, "I'll e-mail you to see how he's doing. Okay fellows, we're on our way to the village. Before we leave Ruthy, do you want a few apples and oranges?"

"Sure, Rahl and I could eat a few of each once he feels better."

Appy took them from the front seat. She placed them in the fold of her over blouse.

The drive to the village proved to be uneventful. Appy dropped off two bushel-baskets of fruit, one from him, one from Father Jeff. Brent looked under the hood.

"This looks good, Ap. I'd still clean the filters before driving a long distance."

"Yeah," Appy answered. "I think you're right."

"*Merci beaucoup*, Ap," Brent said.

Lamar shook hands with Appy and Gbandi.

Appy shook the hand of Brent stating, "The boys seemed to enjoy their excursion and each other. See you soon, Lamar, for the young player's practice."

Appy and Gbandi were happy to be heading home. After all, the day was long and shopping tiring. The boys enjoyed their purchases; time spent with Sarah, and seeing Ruthy again whose cookies were always delicious. However, now it was time to wind down.

Gbandi helped Appy unload the box Sister Jenny sent at the shed. Both thought they needed a twenty-minute nap. Appy brought one bushel-basket of fruit and Gbandi the other to the kitchen. Gbandi told Sister Myra that he needed a little nap. He went to his room. Appy begged her pardon. He did the same.

Later at dinner, Appy filled Father Jeff and Father Reed in on his day. They were glad to hear about the car, the success the three had on their shopping spree, and that the apples and oranges went to the village. Appy told them what the sales clerk said about taps on Zenna's shoes.

Father Jeff laughed, "Smart lady all right."

"Oh yes—I forgot, Sister Jenny, sent a box, which I haven't opened yet. However, I will when I go to work in the shed tonight."

Father Jeff asked, "Hum, what do you think is in it?"

Appy replied, "I'm not sure, but I'm anxious to find out. She usually puts in interesting items like film or maybe newspapers. I hope a little note."

"Please share the newspapers if she sends that," Father Reed requested.

"Sure will, as soon as I finish my morning read." Appy chuckled.

After dinner, Appy went to see how Zenna and the toddlers were doing. Zenna came running toward him.

He picked her up, "I have something for you and Ukita. First, I need to pass cookies out and these little toy cars I bought for the boys."

While the boys were running their cars across the floor, he brought out the shoeboxes.

Appy said, "One pair is for, Zenna, and one pair for, Ukita."

"Oh dear," Zenna said. "Pretty black shooes pease, welcome, tank you."

"Oh **DEAR**," Appy looked at, Sister Myra, "That's a new word—seems to me she has picked that one up from you Sister." The two laughed.

Sister Myra helped Ukita put on her shoes.

Zenna said, "I do!"

"How about I help you?" Appy requested.

"Okeydokey," Zenna popped up on her feet, "Watch Zenna dance!"

She found out that her shoes made a sound, so she tapped and whirled. The two girls pulled each other around dancing it seemed to their own choreography. The two could speak understandable small sentences. Nevertheless, they'd babble their baby talk often. Both seemed to understand the other just fine. Appy mentioned to Sister Myra that Zenna seemed to be putting sentences together quite a bit recently.

"I noticed that myself. She's very bright, listens well."

"I'll miss her baby talk, Sister, but I wouldn't want her talking like that when she's twenty-one."

"No," Sister Myra smiled, "I guess not. She's an adorable girl. I think she'll always pull on the strings of your heart."

"I know that to be true, she has totally won me over."

Appy and Sister Myra watched while all the toddlers seemed busy playing. They were happily contented. Appy had his tape recorder next to him. He picked up the conversations between the children.

Later that evening, after the toddlers were showing signs of tiring, Appy went to the shed. He separated the computers that needed repair from those that operated. He took his pocketknife out and cut the tape on Sister Jenny's box. When he opened it, he could see two helmets, which thrilled him, some newspapers that would please the Fathers, five bats, four mitts, an umpire mask, three rolls of film, and a letter.

"Wow," he thought. *"The teams can really use this equipment. The umpire mask is super special."* Appy opened the letter from Sister Jenny in his room that night. It read.

Hi Appy,

I think the people of St. Matthew's church will never stop bringing in this baseball equipment. If more comes in, can you use it? I hope you'll send me pictures of everybody. Maybe Sarah can take some pictures while the games are going on. I'd really appreciate her doing that. Father Jeff tells me you're looking to adopt a gentle little girl named "Zenna" from Sisters of Amity. I'm so thrilled and anxious for you to bring her home. "Do you think you'll marry, Sarah?" I hear the flu is going around there. Take good care of yourself. Take your vitamins. Drink many liquids. Of course, you know I expect many pictures of you, Sarah, and Zenna.

Sister Jenny

CHAPTER 9

Appy woke in the morning with rainfall on the ground and excitement in the air. He began mentally to schedule his day knowing he'd have to fit in the young player's practice. He'd also enjoy time with Sarah in the evening. He had quite a few repairs to take care of. While watching the news, he had his morning coffee. The computer from the sporting goods store would be a job for Chikae and Gbandi. Of course, he'd pay them the going rate.

Around two o'clock, he took off to pick up Lamar for the practice since Rahl was still under the weather. When he approached, Lamar said his dad was walking the government officials around the village, so Lamar told his mother he was leaving. The two took off for Sisters of Amity. Appy began to tell Lamar about Ladi having her pups out here on the plains. Moreover, he'd probably take Biff for Zenna's dog.

"I'd love to have Keena, but I'm not sure what my parents would say about that."

"Well Lamar, you're old enough to care for a pet, but it does cost money for dog food. Rahl and I will probably have both pups and Ladi neutered, so that wouldn't cost you anything."

Appy pulled in at the shed. He and Lamar loaded the car with baseball equipment to drop off on the field, then circled back to get the drinking jugs, sandwiches, and fruit needed for the day.

"Lamar, I'm glad that young people usually like peanut butter and jelly sandwiches because that's the only spread that won't spoil in this climate."

"Yeah, I like it, too." Lamar replied.

When the children began filling the field, Ajani said, "I'm not feeling good today, but I want to play anyway."

Appy sat down next to him on the bench, "That's brave of you Ajani, but we all have to take care of ourselves. You should sit out on today's practice. There'll be many more practices. Maybe we'll play you more at the next practice. If you like, you can sit and watch the other's practice."

"OK, Sister Clare said I'm too weak to be playing ball."

"Of course, Sister Clare knows best."

The practice went well. Ajani didn't look any the worst when it was over, but he didn't look any better either. He wanted nothing to eat.

Appy went over to Ajani, "Give me a high-five fellow. Go take a little nap. Feel better buddy. We'll see you at the next practice."

"OK." Ajani answered in a whipped voice.

Lamar and Appy put all the equipment back in the shed. Lamar sat in the shed enjoying the computers.

"I'll e-mail my mother; see if she's on the computer. She may want to chat."

"Tell her we'll be heading home soon. I have a date at five-o'clock with Sarah, so I'll take you back when I leave for town."

Lamar stayed using the computer while Appy went in, took a shower, put on dress pants, a stripped shirt, and a v-neck blue sweater.

When the two reached the village, Lamar went in. Appy had a moment to talk to Brent about the pup, Keena.

"Lemar's birthday is in a week," Brent said. "If the pup Keena is weaned by then, maybe she'll be an excellent gift for him."

"You bet, Brent. He will be thrilled! Rahl and I will pick the pup up when it's time to neuter her. I'm simply not sure how old the pups have to be to have that type of surgery, but we'll find out and let you know. Rahl and I will pick up the cost as Lamar's birthday gift."

Appy picked up Sarah at the door of the intern residence. She brought with her a list of restaurants that she found suitable spots to eat, talk, and enjoy each other's company. Together, the two chose "The Lanno House" to eat at because Sarah liked the circular, cushioned bench seats with a high tufted backboard that afforded both privacy and comfort—not such a busy place either, where one would feel forced to leave soon after the meal.

Appy fiddled with Sarah's fingers, "Your hands are so tiny, Sarah. What looks good on the menu, Sweetheart?"

"Yum, I'll have Chicken Marsala with a glass of white wine—how about you, Ap?"

"That sounds good to me, but red wine is more to my liking."

When Appy ate some of his meal, he remarked, "You know, I've never had this before, but it's terrific."

Sarah making small talk, "Yesterday at lunch, Ap, it crossed my mind that Gbandi is a fine young man, would you think of adopting him?"

"Well, if you were to be my wife, I'd probably ask that of you. What would your answer be?"

"Why not, Ap, parents could make a big difference in his life. Besides, he'd be easy to love. He's thirteen now, but in just seven more years he'll be twenty. He could be computer savvy by then—maybe even ready to take off on his own."

"You make it sound so easy, Sarah, but I need to get my own life act together at twenty-three before I can become someone else's daddy. I'm fitting Zenna in my life married or not. That's a big undertaking."

"You're right! Of course—time will only tell, Ap."

Appy longed to know Sarah deeper, "Sarah, tell me about your family."

"Well, where do I begin? My parents were both professionals. They're now retired and travel extensively. They drop in to see my sister Johnna and me once a year at Christmas time, pass out a few gifts; no home cooked meal unless we make it, just a chance to be together talking over our younger years. Not many memories there either since we didn't take dance or join anything that I can remember. Things Johnna and I might have enjoyed. My parents aren't bad people, but they seem to think we should be independent to a fault. It seems like nonsense to Johnna and me. We truly wonder what kind of grandparents they'll make. Because of the way, our parents raised us, Johnna and I will always be close as we live together in up state New York. My sister is a teacher and a good one. She's twenty-six years old, two years older than I am. She teaches high school, an age group that can be difficult, but one that she can handle. We've always felt that we better do well in life; otherwise, who'd look after us."

"Sarah, you haven't had it so easy either. I had no parents while always longing for them. You have parents, but still long for a closer relationship with them. Similar we are Sarah."

"Your turn, tell me about your life, Ap."

"Well, I wanted to belong. A family seemed at the top of my list. I think stability is something I should have been able to take for granted, not a burning desire in my heart. I envisioned myself on my dad's shoulders. Mother baking cookies for me as an after school treat. I cried many nights. I often imagined my mother coming in the gathering room to get me, and my friends being envious big time—and crazy things like; if I died, she'd regret leaving me. I know—if I had told Father Jeff about my desire to be shouldered, he'd have picked me up. However, there you are, you don't feel that someone can love you. No one likes rejection in any form, so you ask nothing in the way of affection. You know, Sarah, all these insecurities are within a child who feels unloved. These children in Nairi are without parents because of a disease. My mother left me behind because she couldn't care for me—somewhat the same situation—no parents to love us. One thing for sure, though, I've had two special people in my life."

"Adoption wasn't to happen when I was young. Father Jeff said there was a period of time when people were just not adopting. When they did adopt a child, a girl was what they seemed to want, which in many cases was unusual Father Jeff thought. My chances of ever having parents were all but gone forever. I didn't brood much over spilled milk, but I mourned for it. I thought of it as a death to family, forever—never to happen. Sarah, in my opinion, every child should have a father and mother. Siblings would be an added bonus. I noticed that children in normal school situations drew pictures of their families and pets. My pictures always had blank faces with no loving pets. I wanted a snake, but that never happened either."

He chuckled. "The stubbornness and insistence of these emotions caused me periods of exhaustion—that'd disappear for a time, but reoccurred when I felt lonely. Activities in any form were lifesavers for me. It kept me from being a dreamer of bad dreams."

Sarah reached over and rubbed Appy's neck. She had tears well up in her eyes.

"Sarah, we should talk about something more cheerful."

"What's on at the show, Ap? Do you know?"

"It's about aliens and war. It sounded interesting to me."

"It would," Sarah said laughingly.

"You know, Sarah, we had a practice session on the field and Ajani who I told you about was ill with the flu. Still, the little guy showed up to practice looking very peaked seeming somewhat unforgiving that he was sick. What makes him so boyish? He exhibits this exterior toughness, but clearly there's an underlying softness about him."

Sarah smiled, "I might call that innocent testosterone."

"Aha, I guess you could be right," Appy replied. "He reminds me of myself when I was a kid. I want to bring him to the States with us to give him a chance at having parents. I believe his tough demeanor is a defense shield. After losing his parents, I wonder if it's a means of warding off any further shock. Not being a psychologist, I can't say that with any authority, but he sure acts like a teen at six years of age. I'd like to see him be a little boy."

"He sounds like a robust fellow, Ap. I can't wait to meet the little guy."

"When we have our next game, I'll point him out to you. Server, may I have a cup of coffee, please?"

"Do you want a cup, Sarah?"

"Sure, I'd like another cup, Ap."

"Make that two, please."

After finishing their coffee, "Sarah we better get to the movie theater. It starts in fifteen minutes."

The movie did prove to be good. Appy enjoyed having his arm around his girl along with a few kisses when the people behind them left for popcorn.

"Sarah, it's good just to be alone with you."

"Ap, I was thinking the same thing."

When the movie was over, Appy and Sarah sat in Appy's car chatting for an hour. He told her about Sister Jenny's box of goodies. How Sister Jenny asked Sarah to take many pictures of Appy and the players. She also requested of him to take pictures of Sarah and Zenna with the film she was sending for that purpose.

"Oh, that's so nice of her." Sarah stated.

"You'll never meet anyone like, Sister Jenny. I know you'll just love her. I need to think of how I'm going to get you two together."

"Sarah…Ruthy mentioned that she was going to put on a dinner for the six of us as soon as Rahl gets better. Father Jeff's salivary glands are drooling for Ruthy's roast beef and potato combo."

"It does sound delicious," Sarah replied.

"Father Jeff says his mother always cooked that dish. It seems like he hasn't had it since his mother last cooked it. Rahl says Ruthy is a good cook. Do you cook, Sarah?"

"Well, with my studies and intern schedule, I usually grab food, swallow it whole, and continue on, but if I had some time to myself, I might like making salads and desserts."

"I like to cook meats and veggies that can be grilled even in the winter on a gas grill. I've never felt that eating should take hours of preparation." Appy added.

"Well Ap, a glass of red wine, salad, grilled meat, veggies, with dessert sounds good to me."

"Sure does, Sarah girl."

Time had passed. Appy and Sarah talked nonstop, but it was time to part company since Sarah had to be at work early the next day.

"Sarah, let me know the next day you're off. I need to plan a teen game. I can pick you up and drive you home."

"Okay dear, I have your e-mail address and will let you know right away."

Appy always had a way of pushing Sarah's hair aside to kiss her goodnight.

He kissed her long and whispered in her ear, "I'll see you soon, Sweetheart."

The sun was just about down. While the rest of the drive would be under a blackened sky, he thought it was a terrific evening.

CHAPTER 10

A couple days later, Rahl e-mailed Appy.

> Hi Ap,
>
> I'm feeling better. Ruthy wants to have you, Sarah, Father Jeff, and Father Reed for dinner. Please find out what day would be good for Sarah. We'll work around her. The rest of us don't have a strict schedule. Rahl

Appy e-mailed back.

> Hi Rahl,
>
> Good to hear you're feeling better. Lamar is having a birthday in a week. Brent wants to give him Keena for his birthday gift. I also volunteered that we'd pay for the pup's neutering surgery. That'll give each of us a dog and a half to pay for. Does that meet with your approval? I need to talk to the Fathers soon about, Biff. I told Zenna I'd be getting

a puppy for her. She said, 'I wuve it, ike I wuve Pap Pee.' I can't help but love her. She's such a cute little thing. I hope to e-mail Sarah tonight when she gets home to find out what her schedule is. Ap

Hi Babe,

Rahl and Ruthy are ready to put that dinner on. The two need to know what day is good for you. I'm missing you, so we should make it soon. I think Keena and Biff are ready for weaning before finding new homes. I hope to get Biff for Zenna. What do you think about that? It's good that we stayed well through this flu outbreak. Let me know tonight, Sarah, what evening is best for you? Ruthy is making the dinner plans around your schedule. Take a nice warm shower. Get some needed sleep. Ap

Hi Dear heart,

Wow, today was a tough day at work; however, more importantly, I spoke with Mr. Cronc this morning. He's elated with your work performance and skills. He talked about Cinnae Hospital sponsoring your baseball team! Of course, I put in a good word for you: Anyway, he mentioned baseball uniforms with an occasional invite to see them play. I bet you're jumping in your jeans since I know I was just thrilled for you and the children. Saturday evening would be good for me for dinner barring any emergency. It's the best I can do. How does that suit you? I think you and Zenna will both enjoy, Biff. I will, too. The dinner seems so far away, but we'll make it, I guess. Tell Ruthy I'm bringing some dinner wine for the table. Make sure you tell her so she can forget that when she shops. I know the Fathers will like the wine I've chosen for this particular meal. I assume you'll pick me up around 4:00 p.m. That'll give us time to have a glass of wine before eating. I'm also assuming dinner will be around 5:30 in the evening. You'll probably drop Father Reed and Father Jeff off at the mission house before picking me up. I miss you too, Ap. After this dinner coming up, we can get together in town at "The Lanno House" to enjoy our quiet time together. I was thinking it'd be nice if someday we take Zenna to the zoo and out to dinner with us after. It'll give us some exciting time alone with her. Oh love, I need to go to bed. Sarah

Rahl answers Appy's e-mail.

Ap,

That was so good of you to think of Keena and to share the neutering expense. What's so good about this is that everyone will get to see the pups as they grow. I'm so happy about that! Let me know when you talk to the Fathers about, Biff. We might be able to send Biff home with you the night of the dinner. The pups will need some potty training. I'm hoping the move won't disturb Ruthy's training process. She just says, "Get outside and do your job," in a demanding voice. They go out when she opens the door. Most likely they're afraid of her. I'd let those pups get away with anything. Good thing Ruthy takes the role of alpha mom. Rahl

Okay Rahl,

I'll talk with the, Fathers. Sarah said this Saturday to pick her up around 4:00 p.m., which would be perfect for her. Sarah says to drop off

Father Jeff and Father Reed before I pick her up—that way they won't have to go the distance. Tell Ruthy that Sarah is bringing some wine that she heard went well with beef. Sarah, as you know, is very thoughtful. She wants to help make the occasion swell for, Ruthy. Ap

The next morning at the breakfast table, Appy brought up the issue of Biff. Father Reed said that he had no problem with Biff being at Sisters of Amity; however, the burden of feeding and training her would rest solely on Appy's shoulders since Sister Myra already had her hands full.

Appy agreed wholeheartedly to those conditions.

Father Jeff chuckled, "Wow, what'll the group at St. Matthew think about this? I guess we could say that Biff comes with Zenna, as it's her dog. Moreover, that she loves the animal very much. She'd be so hurt without her puppy. Then—I'll meet you in the confessional, Ap."

"Hey—you made up that bigger than life fib, not me."

"Of course, Appy, you'll need to pay for his plane fare home."

"Oh, for sure, I'm willing to meet all the conditions we've just discussed. Rahl said that Biff and Keena are somewhat trained, so that's a big help. Now, I need to get him off the paper totally and to the edges of the shed outback where there're some weeds. Zenna and I will walk Biff until he finds a few choice spots where he'll potty. Listen to this Father Reed, Sarah told me that Mr. Cronc is so elated with my skills at repairing computers that Cinnae Hospital is going to sponsor our teams here at Sisters of Amity with uniforms."

"Oh, that's absolutely great!"

"Mr. Cronc also said he'd like to be invited to a few games—that he hasn't seen a good baseball game since he came here from the States. The next time we have a game with hot dogs, we should invite him. How does that sound to you, two?"

Father Jeff said, "Sounds good to me."

"Sounds very good to me," Father Reed followed.

Appy said, "Yes, that's a good way to thank him."

"I'm off to see if Zenna wants to take a walk."

Appy brought his recorder and entered the room to see Zenna and Ukita laughing. Sister Myra spotted Appy watching the two have fun, seemingly not wanting to break in until they were finished giggling.

"Hi, little girls, how's your day going?"

Zenna was so happy to see him. She asked enthusiastically, "Zenna and Pap Pee take a wak?"

"Sure, but first I want you to say hello to my friend, Sister Jenny."

"Hawo, Sistee Jenny." In her next breath, "I did it, I did it!"

She was quite proud of herself. Appy thought that Sister Jenny would be so thrilled with her sweetness.

Appy tried again, "Zenna, can you say that Appy bought you new shoes?"

"Sistee Jenny—Zenna dance in Pap Pee shoos."

"Can you tell Sister Jenny about the doggie you're getting soon?"

"Sistee Jenny, I wuve puppy Beef ike I wuve Pap Pee, I did it, I did it!"

"You sure did, Sweetheart."

Just then, Tobi, Jimi, and the others came close for their treat, so Appy shut off the recorder. He shared his goodies of the day.

After Appy passed out the treats and the toddlers were busy eating them, Appy reached for Zenna's hand, "c'mon." The two went off for a walk before the sun set.

"Zenna, I'm close to bringing Biff home. Every day we'll need to walk him to do his pee pee outside."

"Oh...Beef, pee pee outside?" Zenna questioned and giggled.

Appy wondered what she was thinking. He understood she was just potty trained. He hoped that he hadn't upset the works.

"It's a beautiful evening. What do you think, Zenna?"

"Yep, it's beautifue. Go to Pap Pee's sed?"

Appy let Zenna watch an animated cartoon from a disk he brought from the States. Though she quietly watched it, Appy could see her yawning.

"Zenna, we'll put this on pause—maybe you can finish it tomorrow. You seem a little tired right now."

"Okeydokey," Zenna said while yawning, "Zenna go sleepy."

"Let's go see if it's bedtime Zenna, or better yet, let's go to the kitchen first to have some blueberries, sugar, and milk."

Zenna was soon lying down. Sister Myra said, "You wore her out. I should send some of the evening troublemakers to walk with the two of you."

"We wouldn't mind that, Sister," Appy replied.

The days were long for Appy and Sarah, but today they'd see each other. Father Jeff, Father Reed, and Appy put on their best attire. The three readied themselves for the drive to the mission house. Appy had made up a bed for Biff in the event the time was right to take him back to Sisters of Amity. The two Fathers met Appy out front and exchanged greetings. The trip to the mission house was a talkative event as each had something to say about their computer experiences. Father Jeff had talked to Sister Jenny while Father Reed had watched the news, so the conversation was interesting.

When they reached the mission house, Rahl and Ruthy were there to greet Father Jeff and Father Reed. Ladi, Keena, and Biff were wagging their tails for attention.

Father Jeff said, "Wow, it's great to be loved so much. Come here you girls and gent. Let me see how big and beautiful you're getting."

Ruthy said, "We're trying to teach them not to jump on everyone, but as you can guess we're not quite there, yet."

Father Jeff remarked, "Something smells terrific, Ruthy."

Ruthy answered, "C'mon in."

Appy broke in, "I'll see you guys in about half-an-hour from now. I don't want to keep Sarah waiting."

"Okay," Rahl answered. "See you soon."

By the time he arrived at the intern residence, Sarah was waiting outside. Appy opened the car door smiling-big time. He couldn't help but hold Sarah and kiss her warmly. He missed her so much. He looked around and wondered if anybody was watching.

Sarah said, "Who cares?"

She, too, had missed him dearly.

As they were driving down the main street, "Look Sarah, the theater is having a talent show."

He pulled around. Stopped for only seconds to read and get the e-mail address off the bulletin. Of Course, Appy and Sarah both had Sadie in mind for that talent show event.

They talked all the way to the mission house about Zenna, Gbandi, Ajani, the pups, but most of all how they'd never wait this long to see each other again.

"Sarah, I can no longer be without my girl. We have to make up activities where we can be together, either alone, or with Zenna and the other children. This coming week I should be coming in town twice to the hospital. We can go out for lunch if your schedule allows for that."

"I'll check it, and let you know."

By the time they got to the mission house, the smell of beef was emanating big time. Ruthy, Rahl, and the Fathers came out to greet, Sarah. Appy handed Rahl the bottles of wine.

"Let me uncork one, Ap. It'll help sharpen our appetites before dinner."

Father Jeff said, "Yum, this is good wine, Sarah."

"Yes," Ruthy remarked, "Sarah picked it out because it goes so well with a beef dinner."

Appy and Sarah were happy to see the pups. The two played with them a long while.

"Rahl, what do you think, can Biff go home with us?"

"Oh yes, it's getting expensive to feed them now that they're all eating dog food."

Everyone sat down at the table. Ruthy and Sarah brought the food out; roast beef, carrots, onions, and potatoes baked to perfection, along with a small dish of applesauce for each.

Appy said, "You'd think Father Jeff was having filet mignon, the way he has thought about this meal, Ruthy."

Father Jeff concurred, "This is better! I'd take this any day over Filet mignon—what a great job on this meal, Dear."

Father Reed followed, "That goes for me, too."

"Oh thank you both!"

Appy told everybody about the talent show. He asked them what they thought about entering Sadie. Everyone agreed there was nothing to lose. That she certainly had a voice for it.

"Okay, I need to check with Sadie tomorrow to get her opinion."

Changing the subject some Appy mentioned, "Rahl, I want to go on a safari while I'm in Africa. What do you think about that? Maybe everyone can go."

"Oh," Father Jeff said, "you young people can go. Father Reed and I will watch Ladi and Biff."

Appy returned by saying, "That's a bargain if you truly have no interest in going. I'm not sure about the rest of you, but I need time to save up some money before Sarah and I can go."

"I think," Sarah, said, "that Appy and I should go Dutch treat. We'll get there a whole lot faster."

"Simple truth," Appy answered. "Since neither one of us has hit a jackpot yet, that's not a bad idea."

"Ruthy will look into the cost," Rahl volunteered. "She's very good at organizing things."

"Great," Sarah said, "If Ruthy will do that, since that'd be a problem for me. She'll also need to find out if the tickets have to be purchased in advance."

"I hope," Appy, said, "we can just buy them at the entrance gate. Nevertheless, we'll definitely need dates for you, Sarah. I know for sure I'm not going without you, peaches."

Sarah smiled. Father Jeff winked at her. Ruthy served coffee and hot apple pie with caramel drizzled on top for dessert.

Father Reed commented, "Ruthy, you really put yourself out. This whole meal is scrumptious."

"I made the pie," Ruthy said. "Unfortunately, I couldn't serve it with ice cream because ice cream is mush around these parts."

"It's great without it," Father Jeff said.

When the dinner was over, Sarah and Ruthy picked things up and washed the dishes while the men had a chance to converse about Biff's habits. Rahl also mentioned that Brent wants him to bring Keena to Monday's practice to surprise Lamar on his birthday. He said that he'd bring some cupcakes and candles; and that Kaela would come to help serve them. The evening was getting on. Appy knew he had to get Sarah back.

"Ruthy and I can drive Father Jeff and Father Reed home. We'll enjoy the sunset going down. Biff, can sit on Ruthy's lap."

"Oh, that's okay," Father Jeff, said. "Biff, can sit on my lap."

He was worried about Ruthy's allergies.

Appy thought to himself, "*Rahl always has my back allowing Sarah and I to have more time alone.*"

"Well Ruthy," Appy said while preparing to leave, "anytime you want to do this again—it'd be fine with me. The most I can do for you in return is to make hot dogs at the games."

"Oh, I enjoy that so much, Ap." Ruthy answered.

"Okay you two," Appy said. "See you at Lamar's birthday party."

"Yes," Rahl answered. "See you then."

On the way back to town, the sun was setting making for a delightfully scenic view. Appy and Sarah talked. He had his arm around her all the way.

"Sarah, do you want to stop for coffee?"

"Oh no, I'll save that for our next dinner together. I'm so full. You probably should get back to Sisters of Amity, so they can lock-up for the night. Besides you have, Biff, to walk before you go to bed. I also have a very busy day of rounds tomorrow."

"True, I should go. I'll be able to talk with you via e-mail until I come into town next when we'll be on our own time schedule. Sarah, I think you look beautiful against the sunset tonight."

"You're my sweetheart, Ap. You're the only man I have ever felt comfortable with."

"Ditto, as Gbandi would say. I feel the very same way, Sarah."

The two had many more tender words, hugs, and kisses—then parted for the evening. Appy again wasn't happy for the dark of night and going home alone, but his feelings for Sarah made it all worth it. He, of course, was looking forward to seeing Biff at Sisters of Amity.

Upon returning to the residence, Appy checked out, Biff. There he was in his cage next to, Zenna.

"*How sweet*," Appy thought.

It seemed as though, Father Jeff, apparently was reacquainting the two.

Appy got the old leash that Rahl gave him, hooked it to Biff's collar, and opened the cage while Zenna stirred.

She said half asleep, "Pap Pee, my puppy "Beef" is sleeping by me."

"I know, that's wonderful," Appy, whispered, "I had Father Jeff bring him home for you. I'm going to take him outside to go pee pee before I go to bed. I'll bring him right back and put him in the cage next to you."

"Okeydokey," Zenna said somewhat groggily.

It didn't take Biff long before he was finished relieving himself. Appy brought him back, put him in his cage, pulled the covers over Zenna, and headed to bed. He needed to remind himself that he was responsible for getting up to bring Biff out in the morning...every morning.

CHAPTER 11

The next day when school let out and Sadie came to help Sister Myra, Appy had a chance to speak with her.

"Sadie, when I was in town, I saw a large advertisement on the theater window about a talent show for gifted young people. I naturally thought of your beautiful voice. I'm not sure what the prize is or even if there is one offered, but it would be nice for you to enter even if there's no prize. What do you think, Sadie?"

"Well, do you think I'll be too nervous to stand up there and sing?"

"Why?" Appy insisted. "Everyone at practices and games enjoy your singing. You never look nervous at all."

"All right, Ap, if I'm eligible, I'll give it a try."

Appy had the e-mail address. He e-mailed the theater to gain information on what the contest rules were. He was able to sign Sadie up for the rehearsal where the judges will choose the most talented for the competition. Sadie would need to practice every day. Pull two pop tunes and memorize the words, pick the key she'd sing in, pull the sheet music, and start practicing like a songbird. Still, she wanted to attend all game practices to help Sister Myra as much as she could.

"Sister Myra, I'd like you to be at the rehearsal, too. I'll be less nervous if you're there."

"We'll see. You know I'd love to attend, so I could enjoy your performance. It would make my day!"

Appy and Sadie had to get out to the field to begin practice. She helped him load the car up with equipment. The two took Biff with them. Father Jeff said he'd bring Zenna to be with Biff and Appy to watch the team play. Appy was expecting Rahl and Ruthy to come in with Brent's family. Upon arriving, Kaela went in and brought the cooks the cupcakes. The cooks were now aware there'd be a birthday party for Lamar after the practice let up.

Appy gave Ajani a chance at pitching the ball. The little six-year-old did fine. Appy thought, *"He's a strong, tough kid for his age without much weight on him."*

The practice games were beginning to get interesting. The teens and young players were really enjoying the challenge. There was less chopping at the ball, or running bases incorrectly. It seemed like the young ones wanted to play the game by the rules. When practice ended, Appy told everyone that a celebration for Lemar's birthday would take place in the Sisters of Amity gathering room. Everyone slapped hands looking very excited about cake and drinks. "Happy Birthday, Lamar," the team shouted.

Back at the home, the cooks brought out the cupcakes and drinks while Lamar's mother put a candle on each cupcake.

She said, "We'll all sing "Happy Birthday" and blow out our candles together to represent our unity in wishing Lamar a joyous birthday." Of course, Appy interpreted for her.

After all the candles were extinguished, Lamar's father said, "Lamar our birthday present to you is the puppy Keena."

Lamar looked to be in shock. He said to his parents, "*je t'aime*" (I love you) as he cuddled Keena.

This was big for, Lamar—his own dog. He told his parents, "I'll train her well, feed her, walk her, and love her mightily."

He shook Appy's hand knowing fully well he inspired this gift. The family went home that day with a new member to care for.

Appy, Father Jeff, and Zenna went back to the field, picked up the equipment to bring back in the shed.

"Look Fata Jeff, Pap Pee's sed."

"Yes, Appy works here, right."

"Yep, okeydokey," Zenna said.

Father Jeff and Appy chuckled.

Father Jeff shook his head, "She's so amusing and easy to love."

"Appy, I'll go back to the home while you and Zenna walk Biff at the back of the shed."

Sure enough, Biff liked the weeded area.

"Be good boy, Beef, go pee pee," Zenna said pointing her finger down.

"Zenna, we need to teach Biff to sit, come, stay, and go to his cage. We need to give him a bath occasionally and brush his hair. We also need to buy him a new brush and a nice new boy collar and leash."

That night after Appy took Biff out for the last time, he went right to the cage next to Zenna. Appy could see Zenna putting her finger in the cage. She talked quiet babble to him.

Appy thought, *"She probably wants Biff to know her own toddler language."*

Biff licked her finger. Appy also thought that was a good start for the two of them. He mentally complimented Father Jeff's ability to do what works best.

It seemed as if two weeks passed all too fast. Sadie found herself having lunch with Appy, Sarah and Sister Myra. Having Sister Myra was a win situation for Sadie. The two Fathers and the cooks were standing in for Sister Myra at Sisters of Amity. Sarah complimented Sadie on her hair and dress choice for the rehearsal. Sadie was the sixth person in line to perform. When her turn came, it was a stunning performance. Appy hadn't heard her sing pop songs before now, mostly religious or children songs.

The judges remarked, "We think that was simply beautiful, Sadie. For sure, you'll be a contestant."

When all performances were completed, Sadie got the word that she was a chosen contestant. She heard the theater would put the talent show on in two weeks.

Everyone went home so proud. How wonderful that Sadie was, indeed, a very gifted thirteen-year-old. Sadie, too, was very excited. Appy found out that the prize would be fifteen thousand dollars toward a college degree held in escrow at the bank in the child's name. Everyone was thrilled about that, a perfect prize for a girl who'd graduate from high school in five years. Of course, all were hoping Sadie would take the prize, but there were many good entries. Nevertheless, everyone from Sisters of Amity felt she was the best performer. They'd naturally think that, loving her so much—knowing she deserved the spotlight for her many good deeds.

Appy e-mailed Sarah that evening.

Sarah,

I'm coming to see Mr. Cronc in two days. I want to go out to lunch with you, Zenna, and Sadie.

I wonder if we could eat with speed, so that you could help me pick out a dress and a pair of shoes for Sadie's performance. Sister Myra also wants me to buy something to hold her hair back. Ap

Sarah e-mailed back.

Sure Ap, we can do that. I'll try to get a little more time for my lunch period. One of the other interns owes me since I worked her schedule when she had a commitment she couldn't break. Sarah

Two days later when Appy, Zenna, and Sadie were in town, Appy went to see Mr. Cronc who let him know how much the staff appreciated him. Appy told Mr. Cronc about Sadie's performance—that the two girls were sitting in the vestibule.

"Well, I'd like to meet them."

He was a jolly man. The children liked him. He asked Appy what sizes the team uniforms should be.

"Wow, that's unanswerable when one man is asking another man about children sizes." Both chuckled.

Appy said he'd ask Sarah—that she could put a note on his desk.

"When the uniforms come in Mr. Cronc, we'll have a game with something to eat after. You'll be invited."

"Great, my wife would love to come, too. She's quite a fan of the game."

Appy nodded, "We'd love to have her."

"Sadie, I'd also like to bring my wife to your singing performance."

"Oh, I could use you both rooting for me." She gave him the date.

Mr. Cronc gave the two girls each a piece of candy that he kept in his office for just such occasions. Some time had passed—Mr. Cronc had to get back to work. He excused himself.

Sarah came into the hospital vestibule to meet them. Appy took her and Zenna's hand while Sadie followed behind them to the car. In the car, Appy quickly kissed Sarah and Zenna followed suit.

Sarah asked, "Zenna did you miss me, too? Ap—can we swing to the shoe store first, I think it best to pick out a dress around the shoes."

They did find a nice pair of shoes and some hairpieces. While at the clothing store, Sadie picked out two dresses she liked. She chose the dress that Sarah and Appy liked the best and that looked lovely with her new shoes.

At lunch, the four had a very good time together. Appy was cracking some funny child-like jokes. Everyone was laughing heartily.

"Pap Pee, so funny," Zenna, giggled.

Appy wasn't sure that Zenna understood what the jokes were all about, but he made some funny faces just for her. Zenna loved the fries, took two bites of the hamburger, and drank the cherry drink. After everybody enjoyed shopping and lunch, Sarah regretfully had to go back to work.

Appy informed the girls, "We have one more stop to make at the pet store."

Sadie and Zenna picked out a collar in blue and a leash in blue with white bone prints on it.

"Nice choices girls." Appy complimented.

He also bought Biff a brush and an extra one to give to Lamar for Keena since their hair was on the long side and needed grooming often. On the way home, Appy stopped and bought some oranges and apples. Something he did often at St. Matthew and was repeating the behavior here in Africa. He stopped at the village to drop off some fruit. He gave Lamar—Keena's brush and then headed home.

As the weeks passed, and the day arrived for Sadie's performance, Appy, Sarah, and Sister Myra entered the theater and sat down. Sadie went to sit on stage. Mr. & Mrs. Cronc came in and sat next to them. Chikae, Gbandi, Father Jeff, Rahl and Ruthy liked their seats and stayed where they were. Rahl had picked up everybody from Sisters of Amity since Appy's car couldn't accommodate many.

The interior of the theater had a rounded performing stage with dark purplish velvet drapes that opened and shut by a pulley—a somewhat antiquated theater with a lingering smell of popcorn. The only thing heard was mumbling voices of families who were excited for their love ones to perform. The curtain opened, the contestants each said their name, and took a seat in the front row of the theater.

Sadie wore an ankle length dress in a yellow paisley print with a pair of broad-heeled white dress shoes. Sarah did her hair in the restaurant's lounge where they had lunch before coming to the theater. She put in pretty clips that Sister Myra had bought for her. She also put a thin gold ribbon around Sadie's head and tied it in a bow, with a streamer of ribbon dangling on each side of her head. She was a sweet looking African teen and appropriately dressed for her age.

Appy remarked, "If you were a little older Sadie, I'd be asking you out on a date. You look so pretty."

"Thank you, Ap, but I'm a nervous thirteen-year-old."

"No need to worry like that, you go out there girl like you are number one and sing your heart out."

Again, Sadie was to be the sixth contestant. She was happy to watch the five go before her. She thought everybody seemed so good. When it came her turn, she did sing her heart out. Many people in the audience were standing and applauding. Sadie's people could do no less.

Appy whispered, "Sarah, she blushes like you."

Sadie seemed anxious to get out of the spotlight. She walked down to her seat while the clapping continued.

"Wow Sarah," Appy said. "She's amazing!"

"Oh my, yes." Sarah answered.

When all contestants finished performing, the judges whispered among themselves writing down names. Everybody was on the edge of his/her seat. The judge on the left side of the group stood up. He thanked everyone for coming and entering the contest.

He said, "Every one of us enjoyed your performances. With this much talent around us, this was truly a joyous evening. We certainly wish the best of luck to every one in the future. Without further ado, I am announcing the winner as Sadie Laka."

Sadie looked back at Appy, Sarah, and Sister Myra with a seemingly shocked expression. The three stood as did the entire auditorium and applauded her. Sadie ran to her people. When they were hugging her, the warmth of their bodies helped her feel better as she was shaking so. Two others became second and third runners-up. Sadie was happy to have the attention off her for a while. When everyone moved out to the entrance of the theater, Appy gave Sadie her second bouquet of flowers. He knew nothing about the theater presenting the winner with one, too. Sarah piled the flowers up in Sadie's arms for pictures. Everyone was sure the contestants would end up in the newspapers since there were quite a few camera operators taking shots. Sarah, that evening, gifted Sadie with a gold necklace that had a gold musical note charm hanging from it with the date of this celebratory day engraved on it—something that'd always remind Sadie of her big day on the stage.

Appy whispered, "Oh Sarah that's a well-thought-out gift. I'm proud of you."

Chikae and Gbandi were excited for Sadie's success. Each tapped her on the back. Rahl and Ruthy kissed her with pride. Together, they gave her a money card thinking that if she won, she could buy a frame for a picture of the event. Mr. and Mrs. Cronc also gave Sadie a gift card of money to bank for future singing lessons. On the ride home, Sadie couldn't stop talking. Since she was usually quiet, everybody thought that she was simply unwinding from the evening's event.

Later that night, Sister Clare handed Appy a letter from Sister Jenny that came in while the group had been in town. While resting on his bed, he opened it.

> Hi Appy,
>
> As you know, we named you Appy. You'll always be Appy to me, but I think "Ap" is nice if others want to use it. Oh, I just love the pictures, as does everybody here at St. Matthew. Father Jeff e-mailed us that you were getting baseball uniforms. I bet you're thrilled. I sure would love to see those snapshots, as well. Sarah and Zenna are both beautiful. I hear the relationship is going well between you and Sarah. I hope that my prayers have

helped. Everyone will be so happy to add these two to our family. Zenna makes me laugh so much—no trouble loving her! Father Jeff says she'll be coming home with a puppy she calls "Beef," so cute.

He also seems to think you're getting quite close with the little ones and teens alike at Sisters of Amity. He says Father Reed feels the children seem so much happier with you there. He truly sees it in their eyes, smiles, and mannerisms. I can see that you and Father Jeff are enjoying your experience in Africa. I also hear you're looking forward to going on a Safari with Sarah and your friends. I hope you enjoy the elephants since we always had to remain by the elephants for twenty minutes or longer when you were a young fellow.

Send me more pictures and tapes. I wait for them with cheerful interest. Father Larry is sending something of interest for you. I can't believe that you've been in Africa going on six months already. I hope on my end, that your time there passes quickly. Kiss those girls for me. You take care.

Sister Jenny

CHAPTER 12

Sarah and Appy finally found a Saturday that enabled them to take Zenna to the zoo. Appy wanted Sarah to meet Ajani, so he invited Ajani and his friend, Jabarl. For as tough as Ajani always seemed, he was very soft with, Zenna. The two boys had fun with her.

While at the monkey enclosure with its lacy trees, Ajani said, "Look—Zenna!" As he imitated the stance of a monkey, scratching under his arms, while attempting to make wild jungle sounds.

Zenna responded, "Look—Jani," As she repeated what Ajani did and giggled, "I did it, I did it!"

Of course, Zenna never wanted to stop.

Appy diverted their attention to the cat cage and proclaimed, "Look how huge those cats are."

Jabarl backed up and said, "They frighten me."

Ajani answered. "Not me, I'd give them an upper cut and send them flying."

"In reality, Ajani," Appy answered, "I'm afraid the only thing that I could handle is a pussy cat."

"Hum," Ajani said as if he had a muff in front of his mouth.

Appy was sure Ajani thought he was somewhat of a coward.

Sarah wanted Zenna to pet and feed the goats, so they walked around the bend to see them.

"Oh," Appy said, "My favorite mammal, the elephant, is in the next mountainous enclosure."

Zenna was having the best time feeding the goats, so Sarah stayed with Zenna while the guys went to view the elephants.

The day proved to be the best enjoyment for everyone. Appy enjoyed holding his little girl's hand and Sarah's hand too for longer than usual. He also made contact with the boys by putting his hand on their shoulder while directing them to other animal housing cubicles. By now, everyone's feet were somewhat tender, so it was time to rest on the exit benches before heading to the car.

At dinner that evening, the children enjoyed talking about their zoo experience. They also ordered desserts seeming to enjoy that a bunch. Appy and Sarah remembering Ruthy's apple pie ordered a piece of hot apple pie with ice cream. Zenna ate her own dessert and hit on Appy's plate, too. Appy could feel how Zenna was bonding to him as a parent figure since she wanted everything that was his. He noticed her picking on his plate as a sign of that. It made him chuckle to himself. The children now wrapped up in their own conversation were enjoying their dinner desserts. Therefore, Appy had a chance to talk with Sarah.

"Sarah…Ruthy e-mailed me that the safari cost for the day would run $300 each—that the bus leaves town at ten in the morning and leaves the safari area at five o'clock in the afternoon. The $300 tourist package covers transportation there and back, an open screened tourist jeep with a driver, and guide who narrates the safari surroundings. Ruthy said it includes a box luncheon for each, as well. She also found out that we could buy tickets at the entrance booth."

"That sounds great, Ap, seems to me a reasonable price for the day."

"Yes, I thought it was a good price, also. So now we need to pick a day."

"I need to check my intern schedule tonight. Then, e-mail Ruthy as to what weekend will be good. Moreover, I need to appoint someone to cover for me in the event of a pediatric emergency."

"Okay, Sweetheart—you take care of that end. I knew I chose the right girl because organizing isn't my expertise."

The evening ended with Zenna sleeping on Ajani's shoulder in the car.

Appy said to Ajani, "You're likely to make a good father someday."

Ajani answered, "The boys at Sisters of Amity think I'm a sissy because I like, Zenna."

"Why should you care what they think? Be your own person and ignore such remarks."

"Yea—but that's not easy." Ajani answered.

Sarah and Appy sneaked a peek at each other hoping that comment would influence Ajani a bit. For sure, everyone went to bed early that night. It was the first evening Sarah and Appy didn't e-mail each other.

Two weeks later, the Safari morning was upon them. It looked like the day was going to be beautiful. Everyone was to meet in town before ten in the morning and wait with other tourists for the fifty-mile trip. The bus trip was a great deal of fun as everyone was getting to know where everybody came from. In addition, what their line of work was. The bus driver was hilarious with stories and jokes. It was like a comedy hour—a good start for their safari adventure.

Once inside the grounds, Appy pointed, "Look Sarah that giraffe's neck must be at least 14 feet high. It's more awesome looking to me now as an adult than when I was a teen. It's huge—with a black blotched fawn and cream coat that looks like a puzzle."

"See that over there," Ruthy said. "I think cheetahs are a handsome, slinky animal."

"Yeah," said Rahl. "They look like you might cuddle them in your lap, but an easier way to die might be to bury your head in the sand next to this jeep."

"Wow Rahl," Ruthy chuckled. "I'm not in favor of either of those choices."

Sarah spotted a male lion. She remarked, "That lion has an enormous head. Sure is a scary looking creature. How much of a chance would one have if that beast were chasing you? I'm glad they relax during the day hours. Oh look, its yawning, my...what big teeth you have, Mr. Lion."

Of course, Appy enjoyed the elephants. He had the tour driver stay by them for the longest time.

"We should," Appy said, "throw dust over our shoulders like the elephants do to keep the flies away. Notice how long their eyelashes are, keeps the flies from landing on their corneas. Simply neat, I'd say. What other mammal flaps its ears like that. The ears also fan flies away—magnificent!"

Rahl commented, "You seem to know some things about elephants."

"Some," Appy answered. "I've always had an interest in them. I've also read a great deal on the subject. I even wrote an essay on them in high school."

Sarah let out a slight laugh, "Ap, I had a dream the other night that I married you. And we had many children with elephants as pets that wandered around our home. Every time I wanted to move around, an elephant would pick me up and move me to and fro."

"Ha, ha, ha," Appy laughed. "That's so funny, Sarah. I hope some of that dream will come true." He squeezed her close to him.

The guide pointed out a rhino in the distance, "I'd like to go husk to jeep bumper with that stinking animal. It's so damn freaking mean, always scaring our tourists and guides."

Rahl said, "Best not to try that today, sir. Our ladies are a little cowardly."

"Oh sure," Ruthy answered with a frown on her forehead, "Like you're so brave."

The sun was setting. Nothing was more beautiful than the sun going down in Africa. Appy took pictures all day long, but this beauty would be hard to capture on film. Leaving the safari grounds, the four mentioned that when they reached town they'd grab a hamburger, fries, and a coffee for a fast dinner. They needed to head back before dark since Father Jeff and Father Reed were watching Ladi and Biff and most likely were ready to relinquish their doggie-sitting job.

When Gbandi came to work on computers in the shed the next day, he told Appy that Chikae left today. He said he wasn't coming back to Sisters of Amity.

Gbandi said, "He shook my hand, told me that I was his best friend, and that he was grateful for knowing me. I begged him not to leave because I'd miss him, but he seemed sad about something. He hopped on a UPS truck."

"Oh no," Appy responded. "I'm leaving right now to go look for him. Go tell Father Jeff that I'm going in town."

Gbandi said, "I should go with you."

"Not this time, Gbandi, because I can't be sure of your safety, or if it's going to take me on a long search, or even if I need to get the police involved, but when I find and bring him back; and I will, you'll need to be his buddy."

"Okay Ap, I'll do everything I can."

Appy hunted all day long on the main strip. He asked people in restaurants and shops if they saw a young thirteen-year-old boy who should be in school, but ran off. Just as Appy thought his next step would be the police, he spotted Chikae sitting outside a teen game arcade. Chikae was startled when he saw Appy—not thinking anyone would care about his absence.

"Chikae—what are you doing on the streets, son?"

Chikae answered, "Well-er-ah, it's hard to explain."

"You must know there are strangers just waiting out here wanting to abuse you—make you do illegal things for them; who could do great harm to you if you refuse their demands."

"Well seriously, Ap, who'll love or miss me, my family is gone.... There's no meaning in my life without them."

"Oh, Chikae, everyone loves you at Sisters of Amity. I'd not be here if I had no love for you. Please, come back with me. We'll talk about your feelings. You need time with me and Gbandi to build your skills to make a living out in the real world safely, so you don't have to depend on creeps on the street."

Appy put his arm around, Chikae, "Come home with me, buddy!"

Chikae had tears in his eyes. He entered Appy's car.

"Chikae—this is the right move for you, son." Appy said softly.

On the road home, Appy and Chikae talked about his family, his mother, his father, and one very young sister. It seemed like Chikae needed to share his wonderful memories of them. Nobody ever asked Chikae about his family. He felt that he only ate, slept, and was educated at Sisters of Amity. He was grateful for that, but other issues needed addressing. Appy sensed Chikae missed that feeling of belonging that comes with intact families. He needed to talk. He told Appy how his parents hid him and his sister Reva in the mountains when a *coup d'etat* occurred in the region. They never saw their parents again. Someone else found them hiding and brought them both to Sisters of Amity.

"From Sisters of Amity, foster parents took my sister Reva so that she could have a more normal life as a child. I was happy for her and gave my permission. I hope to reclaim her when I can care for her. Supposedly, she has very nice foster parents."

"Have you seen your sister Reva at all since she went with her foster parents?"

"No, I miss her terribly."

"I must check that out for you. You should be allowed to see and be with her."

Appy lived up to his word. On the weekends, Appy, Sarah, Chikae, and Reva often had lunch in town.

Appy also felt he needed to address the feelings these children were suppressing since staff just didn't want to break into their pain, most likely thinking, they could cause more pain by bringing it to the surface. His next step was to consult Sarah about group sessions for these troubled youngsters.

Sure enough—that same day, Appy received the letter from Father Larry that Sister Jenny had mentioned he was writing.

> Hi Appy,
>
> I hope you like the pictures I'm sending. From left to right these pictures are of the babies: Marna, Bobby, Anna, and Eddie. Thought you might like to see the babies you know so well here at St. Matthew. Marna is walking at 9 mos., so she needs constant watching. The other three are in stages of crawling and standing or sometimes both.

I must say, I enjoyed the pictures you sent me of you, Sarah, and Zenna. I've put it in a frame in my room. You have found yourself two good-looking girls. I'm truly anxious to meet them and your friend's Rahl and Ruthy. Rahl seems like someone I might enjoy with his sense of humor. I hear you and your friends went on a safari. I hope you had a swell time and took many pictures. Sister Jenny is good about passing around pictures, so she'll share whatever you send. What an experience you're having! I'm truly missing you.

Father Larry

This letter made Appy feel good after the day he had just experienced. He sat for a moment and looked closely at the babies to see if he could remember their faces as they had grown so much since he saw them last.

"*Yes....*" He thought. "*I can see each precious baby in a new toddler body. Father Jeff will find this a delightful reunion, as well.*"

He was going to surprise him at the dinner table later. Moreover, it proved to be a big surprise that evening as Father Jeff squint his eyes to see the babies in these toddlers—just as Appy did.

Father Jeff proclaimed, "As much as I'm getting attached to the children here, I still miss those we left behind."

"I understand fully well Father," Appy answered.

CHAPTER 13

On a typical busy work night, Sarah was in the emergency room to care for an asthmatic child. Behind the curtain next to her, she overheard someone say Ruthy Parks. She went to investigate why Ruthy's name came up.

She asked Nurse Ada at the desk, "What's wrong with, Ruthy? My friend's name is, Ruthy Parks."

"Oh no," Nurse Ada said. "I'm sorry to say she died instantly. She's behind the curtain next to your patient waiting for the morgue technicians to pick her up, but you might not want to view her. She's unable to be identified unless someone recognizes a mole on her upper thigh."

"Nurse Ada, I have to sit down. I feel nauseated. I need a bag to heave in."

The nurse stayed right with her until she was able to compose herself again.

"Thank you, you're so kind. Could you call Dr. Reese to take my place, please? I'm shook up. I need to call the people who love her."

"I'll do that for you. If you like, I can write in my nursing chart that Dr. Sarah Henderson is notifying family."

"She only has a boyfriend in Africa. Her parents are back in the States, but he'll be able to contact them."

Tears began to flow thinking of Rahl's reaction to this life wrenching news.

Sarah met the men at the emergency entrance. Rahl took one look at Sarah and knew something was very wrong.

"Where's she?"

"Rahl...Ruthy didn't make it. She fell asleep driving home and hit a disposal truck. She died instantly."

Rahl turned away and lamented, "Oh no—WHAT'S going on? How can this be?"

Appy and Father Jeff sat Rahl down, rubbed his back while he cried in disbelief.

Father Jeff asked Sarah, "How are you doing?"

"Not good, I've heaved a lot."

Appy stood up and moved to comfort, Sarah. Father Jeff went back to Rahl's side.

"Ap," Sarah said. "They need someone to identify Ruthy by a mole on her body."

"Rahl," Appy asked, "can you do that if I go with you and stand right by your side?"

"Yes, I guess," he answered—as he trembled in disbelief.

When Appy and Rahl went to the hospital morgue, the staff opened the slab door, immediately pulling her body out for viewing. Fortunately, a sheet covered Ruthy's body with only a circular opening over a mole on her upper thigh showing. Rahl turned to the staff. He nodded that the mole belonged to, Ruthy Parks.

"I need to puke," Rahl said, "Oh Ruthy, why, why?"

Both Appy and Rahl went to the men's room. Appy was no better off than Rahl. For sure, both were sick to their stomachs.

"Rahl, we need to go to the hospital chapel," Father Jeff said. "Sarah says we need to make funeral arrangements."

At the chapel, Rahl asked Father Jeff, "Why? It's not right that God would allow this to happen to a young beautiful girl, giving her no time to wear a white wedding gown, or give birth to children that might resemble her, or not be able to raise any offspring to adulthood, or even experience retirement and grandchildren."

Rahl buried his head in his hands. He cried for the girl he loved.

Father Jeff put his hand on Rahl's shoulder. In a soft voice full of grief, "The way I see it, Rahl, God can't stop these things from happening, but if you believe in Him, He will give you the courage to work out your grief, speak to your heart's loneliness, and set you on the right path to heal your soul in time."

With all this grief, Rahl was going to ship Ruthy's body home to her parents for burial. Appy went everywhere with him until all arrangements were made. But before Ruthy's body would make this final journey, Father Jeff insisted on a funeral service, so all friends in Africa could find closure with the fact that she was gone—something difficult for everyone to comprehend. Many missionaries that she worked with came to the service. All the children and cooks at Sisters of Amity attended. Of course, all the staff's Sisters and Fathers were there, as well. Sarah picked up Brent, Kaela, and Lamar.

The eulogy was simply beautiful. Appy spoke of his friend's devotion to his girl. He stressed Ruthy's amicable nature and love for humanity. He continued, "How sad this is…." His voice cracked. He knew he had to stop and ended with, "May the angels receive her in their care. Moreover, may God bless everyone here, today."

In Appy's silence, everyone shed tears with him.

The teens made finger sandwiches and baked brownies the night before with the cook's assistance in honor of Ruthy's show of love for them. On this solemn day, they would serve the sandwiches and brownies with coffee.

Seeing the teens serving the desserts, Rahl broke down again knowing just how proud Ruthy was of her treats for the children and said, "Like, Ap, once told me—you guys and gals are precious."

Rahl made his way around hugging everyone. Thanking them for attending. Asking everyone to keep him in their prayers since this loss would bear on his soul for a very long time. When everyone had left, Rahl fell into Appy's arms thanking him and shedding more tears as did Appy, Father Jeff, and Father Reed.

Two weeks passed and Rahl never showed up for practices—usually e-mailing lame excuses. One afternoon, Appy decided to stop by the mission house. He found Rahl drinking at the kitchen table. His beard unshaved and looking haggardly.

"Rahl," Appy said. "This isn't good!"

Appy picked up the bottle and poured the liquor down the drain. He made some coffee while he had Rahl shave and shower. Together they drank the coffee with a piece of toast.

"Now Rahl, do you feel better?" Appy asked.

"Yeah," Rahl answered. "But I'm not strong inside, Ap. I feel like a wet noodle."

"Grab your sleeping bag. You're coming to stay at Sisters of Amity. I hope to see you through this if you give me half a chance and a little time. The old life won't come back the way you knew it, but a new life at your age is a given. I'll not allow you to do this to yourself. Ruthy wouldn't want this either. We all love you too much." Rahl, beaten down with all the negative aspects of this tragedy, wasn't registering one day at a time. Appy packed Rahl's socks and clothes, shaving case, and shoes. He packed up Ladi's food, bedding, and what food there was in the fridge that might spoil, along with Rahl's computer and writing pads. Appy told Rahl that they'd come back tomorrow to pick up his car.

Father Reed saw them coming in. He didn't ask any "whys."

"Hi Rahl," Father Reed said. "We've been missing you and Ladi."

"Appy says, Father, I've been a bad fellow, crying and drinking."

"You're Appy's best friend," Father Reed said. "For now, why not stay close to him."

Rahl's personality was so bruised that Appy needed to lean on Sarah for answers. What to do—puzzled him.

Appy e-mailed Sarah that night after he, Zenna, and Rahl walked the dogs.

Hi Sweetheart,

Well, I picked up Rahl today. He's a mess. He'll be staying here at Sisters of Amity until we see he's recovering more than he has so far. Bringing him here seemed all right with him, so I assume having him close to me and others, who understand he can't pull out of this overnight, is what he needs right now. Oh Sarah, how long does grief last—one or two years? I tell you, I hurt when he hurts.

I'm wondering, Sarah, if you know a psychologist that'd volunteer his/her time with the children to sit in sessions to help us get the young ones and teens to come forward with their suppressed feelings. It might be good to get Rahl involved, as well. Practically in all cases, this could take on a format much like bereavement groups use that'll help the children and Rahl to talk about their individual circumstances and how to handle loss. Ap

Sarah e-mailed Ap.

Hi Ap,

Wow, so sorry about, Rahl. Stay close and help him live day to day. It's so hard! I just received a letter from Johnna. She's coming to Africa. Since school is out for the summer, she'll spend the summer with us here.

I wonder if Johnna could help in these sessions. You know, she has a double degree, one in teaching and a Master's Degree in social work. She'll arrive this Wednesday. She has a good heart. I know she'll help both the children and Rahl. Saturday, if I'm off, we'll come out to Sisters of Amity since I'm sure you'll not mind me driving out there if I have someone along side me in the passenger seat. I've taken heed of your warnings. I'll make certain I have water with me. You'll know if I'm taking too long; if so, you can come looking for us. Sarah

The next day Appy and Rahl went to the mission house to pick up Rahl's car, cleaned up the mission a bit more, and loaded up Rahl's twin size bed so he wouldn't have to retire in his sleeping bag on the hard floor. They went by the village to pick up Lamar for practice. Ladi and Biff came with them. When Lamar saw Rahl, he ran to him and hugged him.

Appy interpreted, "Lamar says." 'I missed you so much. Please, never miss anymore practices.'

"Oh," Rahl commented, "That's enough to make a person straighten out? I won't miss anymore, unless I'm sick, Lamar."

"Where's Keena?" Rahl asked.

Lamar whistled. Out ran Keena to his side.

Lamar commanded, "Keena sit, Keena stay."

Rahl asked, "Did you teach her that?"

"Oh yea," Lamar said. "She's so smart my parents can't get over it."

Appy said, "Look at our two in the car, Ladi and Biff. They're so unruly."

Lamar answered, "I'm not sure about Ladi at her age, but I can help you train, Biff."

"Sounds good to me," Appy responded. He asked Lamar, "Do you want Keena to come back with us to Sisters of Amity?"

"No," Lamar answered. "Go home, Keena. She makes rounds in the village with my dad. He says Keena keeps him company as he stops at every site to see if anyone needs assistance. He seems attached to her already. Of course, I just love her so. She sleeps with me under the covers with her paws sticking out. Every night I whisper in her ear. Her ears perk straight up while she listens. Then she licks my nose and we go to sleep."

Rahl said, "That's cute, Lamar! How do you say dog in French?"

Lamar answered, *"Chien."*

Appy made mention, "Hey you guys, you better stop this chit-chat. I'm slow at this interpreting stuff."

Lamar answered, "Well, I've not seen, Rahl. I truly missed him."

Appy added, "Rahl will be staying with us at Sisters of Amity for a while. You'll be seeing him more often."

"That's really good," Lamar, answered.

Everybody at practice did a thumbs-up…Rahl's back!

Appy patted Rahl on the back, "Help them, Rahl, they've been so concerned and worried about you."

"Okay guys," Rahl said. "Are you ready to play ball!"

The game plays were so good even Rahl was impressed.

"I think it's time to have a game. What do you think, Rahl?"

"Oh yes, I'm surprised at all the improvements. They did well while I was gone. We can get them ready for a game, Ap."

"Okay," Appy said. "Sarah's sister Johnna is coming in town. I'd like her to meet our kids in play. Mr. and Mrs. Cronc and two of the doctors, Dr Reese and Dr. Sodi, want to come to a game, as well. I thought we might serve grilled hot dogs like we did before."

"Sure, why not," Rahl answered. "I'm a doggie fan."

Appy e-mailed Sarah and asked her to tell Mr. Cronc, Dr. Reese, and Dr Sodi that game time is Friday evening at Sisters of Amity with an outside grilled dinner. They're invited. Of course, he mentioned that he'd be thrilled to meet her sister. In preparation of the game, Father Jeff and Rahl went shopping in town for the game food. Appy stayed back to clean up the field while hoping to give Father Jeff the opportunity to see if Rahl wanted to talk about any private feelings. They were to buy food to make potato salad, two cakes, hot dogs, chips, and bottled water, which was always a good drink—a special treat in Africa.

Gbandi and Chikae helped Appy with all the chores. They sprayed the billed baseball caps to eliminate odors and germs, washed the bat handles, and washed the guards on helmets. Appy washed the uniforms in a bucket of water and hung them on a line that he'd concocted. It was a busy day for all. Zenna and Ukita loved splashing in a bucket of water that Appy made up for them. They giggled and giggled as they splashed each other. Soon Zenna was crying that Ukita splashed water in her eye.

"Let me see," Appy said. "Oh, you're okay." He wiped out her eye. "Splash the water at, Biff. Father Jeff says he needs a bath."

"Okeydokey," Zenna answered giggling with excitement.

Gbandi said, "Kids can switch it on and off...for sure."

"Sure can," Appy replied. "Poor Biff!"

Sarah e-mailed Appy Wednesday night.

> Hi Dear,
>
> Johnna's flight came in today. We talked three hours straight. Dr. Reese and Dr. Sodi are coming with Mr. Cronc to Friday's game. Unfortunately, Mrs. Cronc has another commitment. Do you remember the man from the sporting goods store? He's also coming, as well. Mr. Cronc ordered the

uniforms through him and Bill (his name) showed an interest in the team. Johnna and I will be bringing some gum and other goodies for the children. See you soon, Ap! Love ya, Sarah

CHAPTER 14

Sarah and Johnna pulled up at Sisters of Amity. Appy, Zenna, and Biff came to greet them. Sarah introduced Johnna to Appy.

Johnna was all smiles, "I've heard so much about you. I feel I've always known you. This must be your cherished little girl, Zenna, and her puppy."

"Oh yes," Appy answered. "Sarah and I love her very much. Come inside, you'll see the life we lead around these parts."

Rahl came walking in. He stopped to meet, Johnna.

"Wow," Rahl remarked. "Are all the Henderson's beautiful?"

"There's only the two of us, Rahl," Sarah said.

"Well, your parents must be proud to have two such beauties."

Johnna came close to Rahl, took his hand—moved closer to his ear.

"I'm so sorry, Rahl."

"Thank you. It has been a tough time for me."

"Grieving is a difficult process, Rahl, but having good friends around you is most important."

"Oh yes. I love everybody here very much."

Appy mentioned, "We better get out on the field Rahl since the game is about to start. Sister Myra is handling the teams with Father Jeff."

Sarah put Zenna on her lap. Johnna took Ukita, who sat on her lap. The two little girls by now loved baseball. Each clicked their patent leather shoes. Sadie, sang the National Anthem of Nairi. Johnna was impressed. Appy came behind the fence and placed his baseball cap on Sarah's head. Johnna could sense that the cap meant something special between the two of them.

"Ball one, styke two," Zenna said giggling.

Appy kissed her on her forehead, "You root for the teams little one."

When Sarah needed to bring the water jugs up to the benches, Father Jeff took his turn holding, Zenna. Mr. Cronc, Dr. Reese, Dr. Sodi, and Bill had a great time. Johnna and Sarah enjoyed the plays. Of course, everyone enjoyed the cuteness of the young players.

Sarah told Johnna, "Appy also takes a great liking to Ajani, Gbandi, Chikae, and Sadie. I think he wants to adopt all of them."

Johnna said with amazement, "How wonderful that his heart is in the right place. Has he asked you to marry him?"

"No, not yet, but I'm not sure how he'll adjust being without me when he goes home to the States. On my part, I'm sure; I'm positively in love with him."

"Oh Sarah, how wonderful; I'm so happy for you."

Sarah said, "I could cry when I see how close Ap and Rahl are. How they're suffering Ruthy's passing together."

Zenna looked back at, Sarah, "Ceye?"

"No, I'm not crying, Zenna."

Sarah looked at, Johnna. She raised her eyebrows and winked.

"Be good, no ceye," Zenna replied.

"Oh, she's wonderful," Johnna, said cheerfully.

After the game, all had such fun talking about the plays while Appy and Rahl got the fire ready to cook dogs.

"Gee," Mr. Cronc said. "Smells good, I love hot dogs and potato salad."

Appy followed with, "Hey everyone, what do you need to say to Mr. Cronc."

Everybody hollered, "Thank you, Mr. Cronc for the uniforms!"

Mr. Cronc was pleased. He continued to enjoy his meal.

"What's going to happen to the team, Ap," Mr. Cronc asked, "when you leave to go back to the States?"

Appy answered, "I'm not sure, but we're taking twelve or thirteen children back with us. I hope that someone will unite the remaining boys and girls here at Sisters of Amity with the village boys and girls down the road."

Dr. Reese brought his son's computer for Gbandi and Chikae to look at since it was running very slow. Moreover, Dr. Sodi was picking up his repaired computer.

"Appy," Bill said. "I brought you two used helmets that I found in the back of the store for these fine young players."

"Well, thank you so much, Bill. We sure can use those."

Everyone was feeling full in the tummy, seeming ready to pack up to leave for the day. The toddlers went back to the gathering room. The young players went to their living quarters. For sure, everyone was tired out.

At the end of the day, Appy asked Sarah and Johnna if they'd like to go to dinner with him and Rahl tomorrow evening. The girls and Rahl thought the idea sounded good.

"We'll take you to "The Lanno House" where Sarah and I enjoy going. We need to make plans for these sessions that'll help our young with their feelings." "Johnna," Appy continued, "Sarah has volunteered your guidance in these sessions. I hope to call these meetings—Getting to Know Me."

"Oh, that's good, Ap," Sarah said.

"Yes," Johnna responded. "I, too, think that's a good name for these sessions, not scary and absent of a demanding tone. The children should feel at ease to speak their concerns."

The next evening, Appy and Rahl first picked up Sarah, then Johnna at the boarding house in town. While driving to "The Lanno House," Rahl made mention that Johnna was welcome to stay at the mission house for the summer months since he'd stay with Appy at least that long.

"Oh," Johnna said. "That'll be great. I can rent a car and drive to Sisters of Amity for these sessions. It'll keep me busy while Sarah is at work. How much is the rent, Rahl?"

"Oh, no charge, my company paid the rental fees up front for two years. They're not aware of Ruthy or what I'm going through, so I'd be happy if you take care of the place for these summer months. Ap and I can come and secure everything for you. You and Sarah can clean it up the way only girls know how."

Rahl continued to make small talk, "So this is where you and Sarah hang out? This is a nice place, Ap."

"Yes, Sarah and I like it. It gives us quiet time together."

"Sure, I can see why you two need a place to hide. I know kids are your cup of tea, Ap; however, not so cool at times when you want to be alone with your girl."

"Yeah Rahl, living with us you might want the mission house back."

"Could be I'll return faster than I thought." Rahl laughed.

Rahl said that he and Ap would be at the mission house around midday the next day if Johnna wanted to move in then. Everyone agreed that'd work. At the table, the four talked about the game and all the conversations between teens, young players, toddlers, and adults. As the dinner was ending, the server who knew Appy and Sarah well, asked if they wanted their usual hot apple pie and ice cream with caramel drizzle?

"Not tonight," Appy said, "But maybe we'll have something else."

Appy could see a tear in Rahl's eye.

"Sorry Rahl," Appy said.

Rahl remained silent. He ordered a chocolate sundae while Johnna ordered the same. Appy and Sarah ordered a piece of chocolate cake with buttermilk frosting. The dinner as a whole was very good. The evening certainly helped everyone to become well acquainted with Johnna.

The next day everyone met at the mission house. Dr. Reese relieved Sarah on the day shift. She'd work the evening shift in ER for him. Rahl and Appy moved a twin bed from another small bedroom into his sleeping quarters since his room was larger. Johnna and Sarah had shopped in town buying sheets, a pillow, a thin blanket, some towels and washcloths since girls weren't going to use just anything like the fellows might. The two also bought groceries for the week. The men were busy installing two brackets for a 2'x 4'stud

42" long to use as a brace across the only door at the mission house. This bar would prevent a break in. For the most part, it would help Johnna feel safe. The two girls sat down to rest and chitchat.

Sarah mentioned, "It would be nice, Johnna, if I could live here with you, but you're only going to be here three months. It's closer to the hospital if I stay in town. I get to sleep in a little longer."

By the time everything was done, the place looked like it was suitable for a woman to live in.

The next day Sarah went to work. Appy, Rahl, and Johnna sat down together at Sisters of Amity's big table discussing the procedures they'd use to help the children. Two weeks later the group sessions started. Johnna and Rahl had everyone sit in a circle on mats. Johnna informed the children what the sessions were going to be like, most especially, a place where Johnna and Rahl expected tears; while asking everyone to hug the person who had just bared his/her soul. The older children could help keep the younger children relaxed enough to bring their stories forth. Of course, the children needed to tell about their lives before losing their parents, but only if they were old enough to remember. Everyone in the sessions knew what Rahl had just endured. It helped the children to bring out their stories.

Chikae took the lead. He communicated the difficult time he was having. How he felt nobody wanted to talk about his family or the pain he felt due to the loss of his Mama and Papa; how he was just now seeing his sister Reva; how Appy helped him with that; and how sure he was that everyone had a painful story to tell. Acknowledging his fear for the future was something every child in the room could understand. At the end of his life story, the children gathered around him—everyone gave him a bear hug. Johnna passed out suckers. She said that Chikae's story was enough to handle for one day. Everyone agreed.

"Chikae…Rahl and I want to thank you for your candor. You get two suckers."

The children said, "Ahhhhhh, we listened."

Johnna laughed, "The rest of you need to wait until it's your day to tell your story."

Johnna and Rahl got along quite well. These sessions were proving to be good for the children as well as for, Rahl. Even Johnna told her story—just why she always felt she had to overachieve. She told how close she and her sister were, but neither felt like they should be close with their parents, more like friends than family. In one of the sessions, Sadie spoke out letting everyone know that she felt she'd be a good candidate for adoptive parents—not wanting to be a problem teen. However, because of her age, she also felt she might never have a chance at adoption. She often worried about where she'd go at eighteen—what she'd do in the future. As she was ending, everyone came up and circled her with hugs.

Chikae stated, "No worry, Sadie. You'll be a movie star and sing for a living. You're a very pretty girl—why not?"

She chuckled, "Thank you, Chikae!"

In Gbandi's session, he told how very ill his African parents were. How they were at the village until their deaths. He cared for them until the end. He spoke of how Appy was giving him a chance at a good future. How it was up to himself to learn all that he could about computers before Appy left for the States. Everyone moaned at the thought of Appy leaving. As a rule, everybody liked the idea of two suckers, so somebody always wanted to be next. Except for Ajani, who was up next—not to his liking?

He started off, "How am I supposed to know about my parents? I was too young. Sister Clare seems like my mother. I like little kids like, Zenna. She's so cute! I'm enjoying baseball. Jabarl and I enjoyed our trip to the zoo. We should get a bus so everyone can go again."

Ajani finally began to get to the point. He lowered his eyes, "My parents were of white skin. They came to Africa to do missionary work. Somebody killed them by gunfire in the bush."

He stated he always stayed back when they went to do their missionary work. He remembered back at the age of three that his daddy was a good drummer. He played in the band at parties. He said he went with him many times because, he too, could play the drums very well at three.

"I no longer have a drum, but I sometimes use a pad and sticks to beat out silent music."

Sister Clare had filled Ajani in about his parents to a degree, but Ajani remembered all on his own about his daddy being a drummer. He also remembered practicing with his dad. How everybody applauded when he finished and praised him.

"Good job, son!"

One evening when Appy, Sarah, Rahl, and Johnna had met for dinner at "The Lanno House," Rahl told Appy and Sarah about Ajani's surfacing talent.

Appy answered, "Are you kidding me, Rahl—that amazes me! I definitely will look into a drum set for him—maybe a used one will work. I'll call Bill to see if he knows anybody in town with a music shop and a fair price."

"You know," Johnna, said, "Ajani mentioned his birthday is in two weeks."

"Sounds like a winner gift to me," Appy answered.

Johnna told the story that Sadie related to them. How even she had a lump in her throat at the goodness in Sadie's heart. Appy immediately seemed disturbed but was silent in his thoughts while Sarah seemed to understand his pain. She held his hand, rubbing between his fingers, to let him know she was relating to his deep concern. Appy tried not to intercede while the sessions were going on. He, of course, was interested in any areas where the children were not coping well. He also enjoyed hearing how well they were doing. He was in charge of baseball. That kept him very busy. It's where the children enjoyed him the most. Rahl assisted him on the field without much daytime to feel sorry for his love, Ruthy. His friend's hardest time; most likely, was at bedtime when nothing was going on in the dark but his thoughts and memories of his girl. Appy could hear him moan. Rahl often woke up startled in the middle of the night—awakening Appy.

CHAPTER 15

Appy worked on computers from early morning until noon. His tummy started rumbling which usually meant it was time to stop for lunch. He remembered the cooks had mentioned burgers and lemonade, sounding terrific; he wrapped up the morning work and headed back to the kitchen. Coming out of the shed, he spotted an old station wagon coming up to the entrance of Sisters of Amity.

Appy walked up to the car, "May I help you?"

The driver spoke broken English with a bit of Swahili twang. Appy looked at the other man and woman. It definitely crossed his mind with certitude that this man looked much like Chikae.

He thought again, *"That can't be, I thought Chikae's parents were deceased."*

The driver took Appy aside and told him that these people were looking for their son and daughter, and that both parents spent over a year in prison. They have a daughter named Reva and a son named Chikae. They've been searching everywhere since their release.

Appy walked over to the woman. "Mama," he said. "We have your son here. We also know where your daughter is."

She began to tremble and buried her head in her husband's chest crying relentlessly.

Appy shook Papa's hand, "I knew you were Chikae's Papa at first sight, tremendous likeness. Chikae will be coming to my shed to work on computers today after school. Come with me—we'll have a cup of coffee. You need to talk with Father Reed about Chikae's release papers—also your ability to get Reva from the foster parents who care for her."

Father Reed and Rahl joined them. Father Reed invited the three to come and enjoy lunch at his table.

Appy told Chikae's parents that Rahl was a journalist, "He'd very much like to write your story for his magazine."

"Oh yes...yes," Rahl stated, "I'll get my notepad."

Father Reed remarked, "This is amazing for you two and your children. Your son let Reva go into foster care because he thought that best for her since she was so young, but only with the stipulation that he could get her back once he turned eighteen or could care for her properly."

Appy made mention of all the things Chikae was involved in; baseball, computer repairs, and coaching the young teams. He informed Chikae's parents that Chikae ran away recently feeling saddened by the prospect that he'd never have his family back again. The soft spot in Appy's heart for the family was showing.

"Chikae needed to be raised up because the loss of his family struck him down hard. Suppressing it for so long wasn't good. We've been working with him on that. He has a best friend, Gbandi. The two have comforted each other through rough times, separation of families, and friends. I hope to keep in touch with Chikae for the rest of my life. I'll give you my address here at Sisters of Amity and St. Matthew's church back in the States."

Appy began to speak his thoughts, "These uprisings cause so many families to be displaced. Parents can be eating dinner with family one night and incarcerated the next—terrible instability for families and for what—some group's stupid cause."

"Yes," Chikae's Papa said. "We had a good life with nice living quarters, a good community of people to live near. I owned a store that you might call a party store in the States with everyday foods and items that the community might need or want. The town's people could order items out of catalogs from the States. I've started a new store recently hoping to come back around. The children will make everything right for my wife and me. Mama's heart was breaking—mine too. We went wherever she wanted to look. What money we made went toward searching areas and orphanages for our children. We've been searching for a little more than a year!"

Appy responded, "So, Reva is five and Chikae fourteen. That made them three and twelve at the time of your separation. Chikae is now a tall, good looking teen."

"How tall do you think Chikae is?" Mama asked.

"Oh, about 5 feet 11 inches."

"Wow, you said he looks like his Papa?"

"Oh definitely, there's no mistaking that Chikae belongs to Papa."

"There might be conditions as far as getting Reva back," Father Reed explained, "Such as spending a little time with Reva to readjust her to her own family."

"Certainly," Mama answered, "We'll not tear her away from her foster parents until she's ready. Is she in this town?"

"Yes," Appy answered, "Chikae has been visiting her. We've been taking her out for lunch. She's very happy to see her brother and remembers him holding her. She told her brother to stay close to her, to never leave her again."

Appy asked Chikae's Papa, "How far is your town from here?"

"About 50 miles," Papa answered.

Appy looked disappointed, "I wish I had a car that could be trusted for that distance."

Appy could see Gbandi and Chikae rounding the side of the building, heading toward the shed.

"Gbandi, Chikae," Appy shouted, "Come here before you go to the shed."

When the two came in and Chikae saw his parents, he ran to them whaling, "Mama!" "Papa!"

Thinking this might be a dream that he experienced many nights; he approached them and began to feel his Mama's face, kissing her cheeks and forehead, then his Papa's face. Gbandi stood to the side with tears in his eyes as Appy put his arm around him. Chikae's Mama was feeling weak in the knees. She needed to sit awhile, but she wouldn't let go of Chikae's hand. Her tears were uncontrollable, flowing nonstop.

She apologized saying, "I'm so sorry. I'm a mother who found her children when I thought all hope was lost."

"You're absolutely entitled," Appy responded. "But, before you leave here, I hope to see you smile."

She attempted a smile to please him.

Chikae said, "Mama you never had a front tooth missing that I remember."

"No Chikae, I didn't. That happened when the rebels incarcerated Mama and Papa. Someone put a fist in my face knocking me out. When I came around, I was in prison missing a tooth. We'll tell you all about our time without you and Reva. Furthermore, we'll want to know every minute of your life without us."

"I'm sorry, Mama. I'd like to run into that guy again; he'd have trouble eating anything."

"Chikae," Appy chuckled, "I thought you were a nice boy."

"He loves his, Mama," Chikae's Papa chuckled.

Gbandi came in close, hugged Chikae saying, "Hey buddy, I'm so thrilled for you, but nevertheless jealous of your loving family."

"I understand, Gbandi."

"Yea—sure, I know you do. We'll always have that in common."

"No need to worry about, Gbandi," Appy said. "I had intentions of taking you both to the States with me." Gbandi looked at Appy with wonderment, but said nothing.

Mama said to Papa, "We'll need to go into town to rent a larger place with an extra bed for, Chikae."

"Why not let Chikae stay here," Father Reed suggested, "until Reva is ready to leave with you."

"Yes, you can bring Reva here to watch Chikae play ball. Sit with her here to get reacquainted," Appy said.

"I, of course, have never played baseball Papa remarked, but it sounds interesting."

"That sounds workable," Mama, answered. "I was worried about Chikae's schooling in the event we need to stay a couple of weeks before making the journey home, but if he can stay here that'd be wonderful. I hope that Reva will remember us some, so Papa can get home to his store. We have someone who's tending to it right now. However, we can't be gone for long."

Appy made the suggestion, "Since tomorrow is Saturday, Chikae, maybe all of us could take Reva out for lunch. You know how she likes that. I'll e-mail Jill and announce our visit."

"Sure," Chikae responded.

Chikae's Mama went over to Gbandi and hugged him.

"I'm grateful that my boy has such a good friend. I hear that you two have stuck together through tough times. I hope you'll always stay in touch by mail or e-mail since we have a computer also. I'll give you my addresses for both."

"That's great," Gbandi said. "Both Chikae and I know a lot about computers."

"Gbandi," Mama said, "I want you to come to lunch with us tomorrow."

"Oh no," Gbandi replied. "I don't think so, Mama. It's Reva's time to be with her brother, more importantly, with her Mama and Papa for the first time since your separation. How wonderful is that? I don't want to spoil her fun since Chikae and I often cut up more than a five-year-old could tolerate."

Chikae laughed, "Yeah, we two African buddies can act up alright!"

"However, I thank you for the invite." Gbandi continued, "If you have the best of time, I'll be happy for everyone."

Appy thought to himself that the sessions were helping Gbandi with a deeper thought process.

"We'll have a few games," Appy said, "where everyone will have fun. Reva will find friends her age to play with there, although she told me she'd rather play with my dogs—so funny. Chikae take your parents to the shed to show them the colorful desktops. In addition, the computers you repaired recently. Rahl, will you go, as well? Take Ladi and Biff with you to the shed just in case they need to relieve themselves."

Appy at every turn tried hard to pull Rahl into socializing to both gain ideas for his piece on Africa and regain some of his self-confidence. Appy felt that for Rahl to be a journalist, he needed to relate with real people, their circumstances, and coping abilities. Rahl was about to experience that.

Rahl found that Papa rather enjoyed telling him of his trial and tribulations. He thought Papa's story was much like his own: Tragic! Papa emphasized that his stay was in a dank smelling, dingy prison with no privacy or freedom to question his treatment.

"I never knew if my wife was dead or alive because men were in one prison and women in another. I constantly grieved over what might have happened to my children. We had one meal a day, which wasn't very appealing—not more than a bowl full for each prisoner."

Rahl reciprocated by telling Papa about his loss. The difficult time he was experiencing.

With tears surfacing, Papa put his arm around, Rahl, "These horrific accidents are most difficult to take. However, Rahl, you're a young man. I'm sure life will come back to you in abundance. I know you'll find life good just as Mama and I are finding the sweet side of life again. It'll happen for you, Rahl. It's sure to happen just as Mama and I are experiencing newfound happiness with Chikae and Reva today. My family will certainly pray that your new life will come somewhat faster than ours did."

"Thank you, sir. I wish you the very best with your love ones. When I write my article for the magazine, Papa, I'll send you a copy."

"I'd love that. I'll post it on the wall in my store to give others courage who might be searching for their love ones."

The following day, Appy, Rahl, Chikae's Mama, Papa, and Chikae pulled up to the house where Reva lived. Reva came out the front door. She was overwhelmed at the sight of her parents. She definitely knew them. Her Mama and Papa hugged and kissed her. Papa picked her up. He held her in his arms.

"I'm too heavy now, Papa?"

"You'll never be too heavy for me, Reva dear."

When Papa did put Reva down, she moved toward Chikae for a hug.

"We have so much to be grateful for, Reva," Chikae said through his tears.

After the private greeting of family members, Reva's foster parents came out to meet the couple.

"We're so happy for you. Of course, we'll miss her dearly. However, we have five other foster children; and we pray that they too will be as fortunate as, Reva. She has been easy to love. That speaks well of you two."

Mama explained to Jill and Berry that Chikae will stay at Sisters of Amity. Moreover, since they came in on bus, they'd rent a car to take Reva to see where her brother lives.

"He plays baseball," Mama said. "I'm sure she'll like to see him in motion. We need to leave him there because of his schooling."

"Yes, Reva is in school, as well," Jill expressed. "We'll explain her time schedule to you, so that you'll know when she's available for family time. My biggest wish as a foster parent is to get pictures of her as she grows."

"I'll be sure to remember you." Mama said, "Because you cared for and loved our daughter; you two deserve all our respect. If you only knew, how much I prayed that my children were living, warm, fed, and loved. Trust me; we'll never forget you or your husband.... Reva might forget in time since she's so young, but I will never—I promise you that!"

With tears, the two hugged each other.

Appy decided to check his computer upon arriving home to see if Sarah had e-mailed him.

Hi Ap,

I'm so excited for, Chikae. How marvelous for him and his family. I cried out of joy. I talked to Bill from the sporting good shop. He gave me the address of a music store that takes in second hand instruments as a trade in for a new one. Maybe you and Rahl can pick-up Johnna and come in town for lunch. Later, the three of you can go to the music shop to look for a used drum set. At least you will get an idea of cost and type of drum that'd be good for Ajani. I'm anxious to see how well Ajani plays the drum. His innocent testosterone might work well when playing drum, tsk, tsk. I definitely think he'll be excited about his birthday gift. Let me know game days. I'd like to see how Chikae's parents react to the U.S. game of baseball. Darn, Johnna is having more fun than I'm having with my intern schedule. Sarah

Appy shut down his computer. He went inside to get Zenna for breakfast.

"Little girl after breakfast, Rahl and I will take you on a nice walk down the path that goes pass the school onto the playground. We'll take Biff to practice some of Lemar's dog training techniques."

"Yep, Beef smart, I wuve Beef."

"Go wake up Rahl, Zenna."

"Okeydokey," As she walked to Appy's bedroom, poked her head in the door, "Wah, Pap Pee go wak."

"Okay Zenna, I'll be right there."

Biff and Ladi both liked the walks and Biff was training very well. Rahl would call Biff "COME." Give him a treat. Then, Appy would do the same. Give him another treat. Biff was learning the word "COME" very well while Ladi was getting treats without following any commands. With repeat and treat, soon Biff would know some English.

Zenna, followed Biff around saying, "Be good boy, pee pee Beef."

"Aha," Rahl said, "she knows the most important training element."

"C'mere Biff," Appy took thorns from his ear. "Biff," Appy complained. "What picker bush did you run into?"

"Oh no, Beef has boo boo?" Zenna cried.

"He's okay, Zenna," Appy answered.

Appy told Rahl about lunch with the girls. That he also wanted to shop for a drum set while in town.

"Sounds nice to me, Ap—I'm learning from the sessions to do things as they come and not to think about the negative aspects of my life—hard, but doable. With Johnna here, I'm not totally alone, or feeling like the only third wheel between you and Sarah."

"Rahl—neither Sarah nor I want you to think that way right now." Appy chuckled, "We'll know when it's time to back you off."

"Yeah, you two are the best."

"Zenna, honey," Appy asked, "are you getting hungry for lunch? Let's get back, so we can find out what the cooks are making."

Rahl asked, "What's your favorite lunch, Zenna?"

Zenna answered, "I ike fies."

"Oh, I like French fries, too, Zenna. I guess everyone does." Rahl replied.

"Goodness Gacious, I wuve fies." Zenna said with a serious look.

"Zenna, you're turning into a little nun," Appy frowned. "I need to talk to those ladies."

Zenna giggled, "Fies good."

Rahl whispered to Appy, "That's so damn funny!"

Both tried very hard to keep their composure.

CHAPTER 16

After lunch, Appy e-mailed Sarah but was sure she wouldn't read it until evening came around when off work.

Hi Sarah,

Johnna, Rahl, and I are coming in town tomorrow. I'm also anxious, like you, to see what Ajani can do on the drum. I'm going to get a baseball game going for Ajani's birthday. Chikae's parents and Reva want to come to Sisters of Amity to see the game, so I'm thinking the day after tomorrow, Saturday when school is out. I hope you'll be off. I need to get that drum set tomorrow. I'd like a drum with a cymbal that works by the player's foot. We'll see what they have in the store that might be suitable for him—some kind of combination that I can afford. I miss you every day. I, too, wish you had the summer months off like, Johnna! I especially wish I could be there to give you a good night kiss. See you tomorrow, love. Ap

At lunch the following day, Rahl was extremely hungry. "I'm going to have a fat hamburger smothered in onions with tomato, cheese and lettuce on top, yum."

"Wow, that sounds good," Appy, agreed. "I'll have the same with coffee."

"Me too," said Rahl, "coffee please."

The girls decided to order the same with chips and a lemonade drink.

"Are you finding any new revelations in your sessions, Johnna?" Appy asked.

"Not right now, but they're wonderful with their stories and their feelings."

Appy continued, "Rahl tells me that he's learning from the sessions, too."

"I hope so, Rahl," Johnna commented. "Who better to learn from than innocent children who've a tendency to wear their feelings on their sleeves?"

"Sarah," Appy said, "listen to what Zenna said to Rahl and I yesterday," 'Goodness gacious, I wuve fies.' Appy with laughing tears, "Rahl and I have wanted to laugh our hearts out, so now we can."

While still in deep laughter, Rahl said, "The Sisters are corrupting the poor little thing."

"Ahhh, she's such a sweetheart," Sarah remarked.

It was hard to come out of the laughing mode, but Appy wanted to plan the next game to be a big event. He wanted the suggestions of all. Johnna said she'd bring a few blocks of cream cheese and a sweet cherry salsa as a topping to spread on butter crackers for an appetizer. She felt sure the children would love it.

"Yummy," Sarah remarked. "That sounds delicious, Johnna."

Appy said he'd e-mail Brent and invite his family to the game and dinner. Rahl and Appy mentioned that they'd be responsible for the hot dogs and chips. Father Jeff had already volunteered to purchase the birthday cake.

Appy related, "Father Jeff likes to be the important one at birthday parties. Bless his tenderness."

Of course, Sarah said she'd bring bubble gum, "I think the children would also like lemonade like this. How about you Johnna, do you think so?"

"Yes," Johnna answered. "It'll quench their thirst. Moreover, it doesn't necessarily need to be cold to taste good either."

"Sarah," Appy interjected. "I think Sisters of Amity has some large mugs you can use."

"I also have some at the mission house," Rahl added.

"Sarah girl," Appy asked, "would you e-mail and ask Bill, Mr. and Mrs. Cronc, Dr. Reese, and Dr. Sodi to come and join us, too?"

"Sure, I'll do that, Ap."

"Good, I think we planned that out fairly well," Appy praised everyone. "I hate saying this, but it's time to get Sarah back to the hospital." Appy walked Sarah to the rear entrance door. "Sarah my lips are yearning to kiss you, but without an audience. I'll e-mail you tonight, and see you tomorrow."

"Okay Ap, just a little kiss will do for now." A little peck and they parted company.

Johnna, Rahl, and Appy needed to do some shopping for tomorrow night's grill out. Most importantly, he needed to go to the music store first to see if Ajani's drum was even a possibility. Appy went up to the owner. He introduced himself. He asked him if he had a used drum for a little six-year-old child.

"Oh, Bill told me you'd be coming in. He asked me to take good care of you. My name is, Ari. It's good to meet you. I have a few drums that are used and are in the storage room. Most often, the children drive their parents crazy with them and they come back for a refund. Come in the back, I'll show you what I have."

"This little boy's name is Ajani," Appy said. "We've just found out that he plays well. His father was doing missionary work here, but also played the drum at parties. Ajani says he played with him at times."

Ari said amused, "I know of this father and son combo. I believe the boy was only about three at the time. He could play the drums much like his father. He was just darling, very robust, and a perfect entertainer."

"Ajani's parents," Appy said, "regretfully were killed in the bush. Ajani is now living at Sisters of Amity."

"I'm really sorry to hear that. What a waste of talent. He was also an exceptionally delightful man. We talked at great length. I never met his wife. I saw them at a wedding and a celebration of an anniversary. I spoke with the father on both occasions. After playing with his father for a few songs, the boy disappeared, maybe taken by his mother, and probably brought home and put to bed. He was good enough and sweet enough to receive a standing ovation and applause."

"Wow, Ajani has been telling us about such occasions in session," Rahl commented.

"Yes," Johnna concurred. "He surely has. We thought maybe he was exaggerating a little, but I see that's not the case."

"I was thinking of a drum with a cymbal that you operate by foot," Appy informed the owner.

"Oh yes," Ari replied, "Ajani plays the cymbals well, but he doesn't need a foot pedal. He's fluent with drumsticks. I have the right combination for your needs."

He showed them a nice set. The owner reduced the price even more since he knew the father. He most likely felt he'd be helping the father's son. Appy told the storeowner about the game that was coming up with a birthday party for Ajani afterwards.

"Ari, we'd love to have you attend."

"Yeah," Rahl said. "We'll be slapping together a light dinner and cake."

"You know, I'd like to hear that little guy play once again. Maybe Bill and I will come together. We folks who originate from the States love baseball, but football and boxing tend to be much more popular around these parts. I've truly missed baseball."

Saturday morning Appy was up early. It looked like a very nice day for the game. Last night it had rained a little bit. The air felt clean of dust and fresh. Zenna woke up in a good mood, also. Appy had told her about the game and Ajani's birthday party. She, of course, would get to watch the game on Sarah's lap. Her Pap Pee had also told her that she could play with Ukita and Reva after the game ended.

"Zenna, sit here and have some breakfast with me. I'll make you some chocolate milk, cereal, and maybe you can have a slice of my toast with jelly."

"Yep, pap pee I ike that, tank you."

"*Gee, she found the right word,*" Appy thought to himself. "After breakfast Zenna, we'll get Rahl up to take Ladi and Biff for a walk."

"Okeydokey," Zenna's favorite word and one she used often.

Just then, Rahl walked in the kitchen, "Rahl, you're up early this morning."

"I was too excited to sleep in."

"Yeah, I know what you mean."

"We need to walk the dogs Rahl, so I can get started bringing the equipment out on the field."

"Okay, I'll just grab a donut and cup of coffee. Then, I'll be all set to go. What time is the game to start, Ap?"

"Around three o'clock, which is a little bit earlier than usual since its Saturday. We'll grill dogs about five o'clock."

"Sounds good to me," Rahl said.

Around two o'clock in the afternoon, Sarah and Johnna brought Kaela, Brent, and Lamar to the entrance of Sisters of Amity. Appy and Rahl were out on the field laying down bases and setting up the baseball equipment. The girls enjoyed talking with Sister Myra and the toddlers. Brent walked to the field with his son, Lamar.

Kaela picked up a baby girl, "me *be'be'*."

"Oh," Sarah said, "Kaela has learned an English word—me."

Kaela continued, "Sarah, me *be'be'*."

Sarah went over to Kaela; put her hand on Kaela's arm, "Wait for, Ap, to come off the field, Kaela."

Kaela sensed Sarah didn't understand. She'd wait for, Appy. Of course, Zenna was overjoyed to see, Sarah. Sarah picked her up and bear hugged her with kisses on her neck. Zenna giggled, "Again!"

Father Reed and Father Jeff were with the cooks making up lemonade in lots of jugs.

"Father Jeff," Sarah said, "the birthday cake is so cute."

On top of the chocolate icing, was a seven with a colorful drummer dressed in blue and white stripped trousers, and sporting a baseball cap on his head with a pair of drumsticks in his hands.

"That's absolutely sweet for, Ajani," Johnna said.

Ajani wasn't to see his cake until Rahl brought it in. At that time, Appy would bring his drum and cymbal in behind him.

Mama, Papa, Reva, Bill, Ari, Mr. and Mrs. Cronc, Dr. Reese, and Dr. Sodi rolled in one after the other. Sister Clare brought the young players out to the field. The teens were on their way. Sadie, on the job as usual, handed each player a bottle of water. Chikae and Gbandi would be assisting the outfielders by standing a distance behind them. Mama and Papa would be able to see Chikae and Gbandi in their leadership role today. Tomorrow, the teens would play a game so Mama and Papa could watch their boy at the top of his game, but this day included good conversation, good food with friends, and most importantly a birthday party for a precious little boy.

As the game was starting, Zenna sat on Sarah's lap—Ukita on Johnna's lap. Clicking their shoes had become a game cheer of sorts for them. Johnna seemed comfortable with Ukita who was much like Zenna in sweetness. Kaela held a small child. The child babbled. Sarah, Kaela, and Johnna smiled because the child was very comfortable with Kaela's French. Appy came around the fence and put his cap on Sarah's head.

"Ap," Sarah gestured. "Listen to what Kaela is saying about *be'be'*."

"She says she wants to adopt a baby girl and asks if we could help Brent and her do that?"

"My goodness, Ap, I'm so surprised—when do they want to do this?" Sarah asked.

"ASAP," Appy replied smiling.

Sarah was so excited. She went to Kaela, hugged her saying, "Oh, for sure!"

"We'll talk about this later Sarah with Kaela and Brent," Appy added. He hurried back to the field.

Today Ajani had the honor of hollering out "batter up" since it was his birthday. He certainly hollered louder than Appy or any of the other boys.

"Ajani you're going to have a sore throat tomorrow," Appy chuckled. "You darn near scared the pants off these guys."

Rahl sat on the bench with the young players clapping, "First team up!"

The men all chatted about the game and players. Mama and Reva watched the game with interest. Reva played a little with Zenna and Ukita as the two sat on Sarah and Johnna's laps. Reva sang "Teeny-weeny Spider" and animated the spider with her hands. Everyone could see the two toddlers were trying out the movements with their little hands, too.

Sarah thought, *"If I want to be a good mother someday, I need to get that song on paper."*

Papa especially thought the game was enjoyable. Everyone hollered and screamed until they were hoarse. Just as the game was ending, Ajani hit a home run. That excited everyone all over again.

Appy slapped him on the buttocks, "Happy Birthday, Ajani!"

Ajani threw his cap in the air. All the team gathered around him to congratulate him. Just then, Chikae and Gbandi lifted him in the air, put his cap back on, and carried him back to the bench.

Zenna, was hollering, "Home won Jani."

"Yes, Zenna a home run—everybody is happy." Ajani shouted loudly.

He came close to, Zenna. Put his cap on her head. Appy loved the admiration they had for each other. He winked at Sarah knowing fully well that Ajani had witnessed him placing his own cap on Sarah's head many times.

Appy and Rahl cooked the hot dogs. The women poured lemonade. Mrs. Cronc had made a cold, black bean spaghetti salad with little sliced cherry tomatoes, sliced black olives, topped with ground black pepper and Italian dressing. It was good, eaten very fast, but there was enough for everyone to enjoy. Of course, Johnna's cream cheese blocks with cherry salsa topping and butter crackers were gone in a flash. Both children and adults enjoyed that touch of sweetness.

After eating, Rahl brought out Ajani's cake.

"Oh," Ajani said. "I see my story about drums has become me on my cake. It's cute, thank you."

Appy came up behind him. "Ajani, do you think you could play this?"

Ajani turned around swiftly.

"This is my birthday present to you."

Ajani's eyes welled-up. He hugged Appy, "You're the next best thing to my own daddy."

Appy was proud that Ajani could express the soft side of himself. It certainly was meaningful progress. Ari came close to, Ajani. He related to him that he came all the way to hear him play. He told Ajani about knowing his dad. How he enjoyed their music together immensely.

Ajani gleefully said, "Gee, I like this drum." He stood next to the drum. Fiddled with the drumsticks trying for the feel he once felt. He began to play slowly. His face beamed with the rhythm of the sticks.

Everyone thought that his warm up was as good as it could get, but when Ajani began to master the drum again, the crowd was astounded. He played that drum and cymbal like a pro.

"Ajani, I like the beat of a marching band." Appy asked, "Can you play some marching music for me?"

"I'll try." Ajani nodded in compliance.

"Rahl, please bring Ajani's drum and a chair to the entrance door."

Appy signaled the young players, teens, and toddlers to come outside, get behind him and march. Zenna, Ukita, Tobi, and Jimi were jumping and stomping their feet all over the place. It looked like an Indian powwow with great clouds of smoke. Ajani giggled while he played as he watched how much fun everyone was having. Sister Clare had a frown on her face thinking about the cleanup of these children.

"Dust off kids before you go back into the gathering room, Okay?" Appy hollered.

This was a big day for all. It was beginning to end around eight o'clock with Ajani's cake. The crowd gathered inside the large room to eat cake and avoid the flies that were out in abundance absorbing the succulent odor emitted by the grilled hot dogs. The adults ate their cake on the kitchen tables along with as many teens as chairs to seat them while everyone else sat on mats in the gathering room. The lemonade was very enjoyable with the hot dogs, but Sarah and Sadie both thought the sweet cake made the lemonade tart, so they passed out bottles of water to the children. The adults enjoyed coffee. Both Sarah and Sadie learned one thing, no lemonade drinks when serving desserts. Everyone sang "Happy Birthday" to Ajani. He beamed with sweetness.

After the party and most everyone had left, Ajani cleaned and packed up his drum and cymbal putting it in Appy's shed; where Appy thought he could practice without bothering the sisters. Sarah, Appy, Ladi, and Biff walked with Sister Clare and the children back to their sleeping quarters. Sarah was going to stay with Johnna at the mission house this night, so they could come in for the teen game the next day together.

On Sunday, Appy picked up Sarah and Johnna at the mission house. He brought the two and Lamar in for the teen game. Chikae's parents and Reva were coming in to watch the boys and girls (especially Chikae) play. They'd also have lunch with Father Jeff and Father Reed. Jill had called Father Reed with "deserving news." He felt lunchtime would be a perfect time to go over the information. Appy gathered the teams around him.

"Let everyone make this a splendid game for Chikae's parents. As you know, I never care who wins, but play with your whole heart. Chikae will be leaving us soon, so play this one for him."

The teams clapped that musical sound again. *"Where did that sound come from?"* Appy thought.

Zenna and Ukita enjoyed a second day of play. Zenna put her arms backwards around Sarah's neck, "I wuve you Sarah and I wuve Pap Pee, and Beef."

Sarah answered, "Yes, we love each other this much." She put her arms in a big circle.

"Yep, that big," Zenna replied.

"Wow, how about that angel!" Johnna remarked.

In the end, chikae's team happened to win by one run, which Sadie hit. Rahl, Appy, Gbandi, and Chikae picked up the equipment and brought it back to the shed. The lunch the cooks prepared was spaghetti sauce made with chicken and mushrooms over pasta, salad, homemade garlic rolls with butter, coffee and left over birthday cake for dessert. When the women cleared the table, Father Reed told Mama and Papa that Jill and her husband felt Reva was ready to go home with her parents. Jill also said she could have her packed and ready by tomorrow if that suited the two of them.

"Chikae," Mama asked, "Can you be ready by tomorrow to make the journey home? Papa should get back to work."

"Sure," Chikae said, "I've very little to pack—just some clothes and shoes. I'd really like a bat with all the boys and girls names on it."

Appy responded, "I'll make that happen, Chikae."

The following day was bittersweet for most everyone, but each promised to write to Chikae often. Chikae also promised to e-mail Appy and Gbandi, especially when Papa's machine needed repair.

The children's sessions were also coming to an end as school would begin within two weeks back in the States where Johnna would have lesson plans to go over. She and Rahl had come to know each other quite well through these sessions—each had a great deal of respect for the other.

"Johnna, when I get home at the end of this year, I'll look you up. I should be ready to date by then."

"Okay Rahl, I'll hold you to that."

"You should be making great strides by then, Rahl. If I'm still available," she chuckled, "I'll be happy to have a cup of coffee with you."

Appy and Sarah also talked to Father Reed about Brent and Kaela's chances of adopting a baby girl.

"I believe," Father Reed, said, "That because we know them well, and Kaela is on medication to ward off any further illness, they'll be eligible to adopt. This couple will give a child a loving home."

Brent and Kaela wanted a child who came from the parents who died at the village. That made sense to them. The little girl that was sitting on Kaela's lap during the game was to be the chosen child. Brent and Kaela renamed the ten month old, Nettie. Lamar and Keena were very gentle, somewhat protective of the baby. This family was the happiest they'd been in a very longtime. Appy and Rahl covered the cost with Sisters of Amity without the couple's knowledge. The board of contributors was happy with a reasonable fee, which would cover some of the cost of food needed to keep the orphan home open and operating for the remaining children. Father Reed also made it clear to the board that all children adopted by the Nairian people should get a break in the cost since it could encourage others to take responsibility for their country's children.

CHAPTER 17

A year had passed. Appy was busy with his teams, caring for Zenna and Biff, and dates with Sarah. This excursion to Africa would always be highly remembered both as the best experience because of meeting his love and the people of Africa and worst because of Ruthy's passing and Rahl's slow recovery. Rahl had written his dad about Appy's abilities and his extremely close relationship with his cherished friend. Rahl's father, Oliver Clarkston, knew about Rahl's traumatic experience. How Appy pulled him through the worst experience in his son's life. He was happy to accept Appy's re'sume' promising him a top-notch position upon arriving in the States.

He related to his son, "Lucky for, Ap, that I'm opening a large plant in West Branch. He'll fit in perfectly. I think this is a location that'll make him happy."

Of course, that elated Appy and Father Jeff. To Father Jeff, it was like a dream come true. It meant everything to him and Sister Jenny that everyone could continue on much like an extended family. Appy would have needed to travel everyday from West Branch to Saginaw and back just to have a home near St. Matthew. Moreover, that length of time commuting would leave him exhausted at week's end. Being at the new plant would suit him fine. He was simply overjoyed.

Appy had an important date with Sarah for dinner at "The Lanno House." Time was fleeting. Appy knew it was only three months before departure for home. He thought about leaving, Sarah. The thought was haunting him. He had no more time to put it out of mind. Sarah wore a striking wrap-around-dress with hot pink, turquoise, and purple splashes of color that made a very rich and gorgeous looking outfit.

Appy mentioned, "Sarah, you look especially beautiful tonight."

"Thank you, Ap," Sarah answered.

"How would you like some wine and pasta? Appy asked.

"Yes, that sounds good. I haven't had pasta in a long time."

Toward the end of the dinner, Appy looked adoringly at his girl.

"Sarah," Appy spoke softly, "I love you. I love your ponytail, the ease in your appearance, and in a room full of people, you'd catch my eye. Do you remember I found myself unable to speak the first time we met? He ran his fingers through her hair and stared into her eyes. I thought your reddish brown hair and sparkling blue eyes were stunning, but I couldn't get a word out. I love that you are completely comfortable with children; moreover, speak to them in an intelligent, quiet manner; that you look perfect in a baseball cap; and the smell of lavender in your hair just turns me on."

He kissed her on the chin, nose, and forehead.

"Sarah, will you marry me?"

"Oh Ap, your words to me are always so beautiful. I love you, too. Yes, of course, I'll marry you."

They cuddled and kissed hoping the server wouldn't come for their dessert order just yet.

"I realize Sarah that you'll need to stay in Nairi for six months longer than I, but we'll correspond by e-mail and through letters. I'll be busy working for Rahl's father in his new West Branch plant. Sarah, what do you think about adopting Zenna, Sadie, Gbandi, and Ajani once we're married, so I can establish the six of us in a nice home when I get back to the States? I can't leave them behind Sarah. They've touched me so."

"Well daddy, we'll really have to budget with a family that size at our age," Sarah chuckled, "But I also love these children, dearly—that's all that's needed to make this work."

"Sarah, the children and I'll need to find things to do together, so that missing you won't hurt so much. Girl, I wasn't planning to fall in love before I had the means to care for a wife and family. Who'd guess I'd meet the love of my life in Africa."

Sarah replied, "I doubt that many couples have a plan. I think love just happens. Other things will develop by working together. Together, Ap, that sounds so good."

"Yes," Appy answered. "I truly love you, Doctor Sarah. You're everything I've ever dreamed of."

"Sarah, I'd like to get married as soon as we can here in Africa. What do you think of that?"

"I think we should talk with Father Jeff to see if he'll marry us?"

"Okay Sarah, we should invite him to have dinner with us and discuss this."

"Yes, Ap, he's a very important person in your life—now in mine. The children love him, as well. Zenna thinks of him like a grandpa."

"I think you're right, but he doesn't seem to mind. She comes with me. That's all he cares about."

"Sarah, I'm for you."

"Oh Ap, you're for me!"

The two hugged and kissed again—then, ordered dessert. The whole evening was everything Sarah had hoped and dreamed of since the very day she met, Appy.

The next day Appy invited Father Jeff out to dine at "The Lanno House" with Sarah and him that very evening. Father Jeff was delighted to accept the invitation to "The Lanno House" since he'd overheard Johnna and Rahl mention what a nice place it was for dining.

While seated in the restaurant, Appy asked, "Father will you have some champagne with us?"

"Certainly, that sounds good, Appy."

Appy and Sarah each had a flute of champagne served to them, as well. While sipping their drinks, Appy told Father Jeff that he proposed to Sarah. However, Since he only had a few months left in Africa, they'd like him to officiate their wedding as soon as they have some plans together. Father Jeff stood up, shook Appy's hand, and kissed Sarah. The three raised their glass of champagne, clicked them together in celebration.

"Oh, you can't imagine how happy I am to hear this. Sarah, I've always felt that you were perfect for Appy," Father Jeff added.

"Well, I think he's perfect for me," She replied.

"I love you both, dearly. Of course, I'd love to officiate at your wedding."

"Brace yourself Father," Appy said, "for what you're going to hear next. Sarah and I want to adopt Zenna, Ajani, Gbandi, and Sadie before I leave."

"Oh my, you weren't kidding about having a large family, Appy. How do you feel about this, Sarah?"

"Well, Ap, and I talked this through. We concluded we couldn't live without them. Of course, they should be our children. We find them adorable and love them, dearly. There were many others who deserve parents, but we chose these children."

"Sarah, you're an extremely brave young woman. I don't think that'll be a problem with Father Reed," Father Jeff said, "Since we've been praying for parents for all these children in Africa. It's wonderful that you have a job to go back to, but if need be, we'll keep the children at St. Matthew until you find housing for your family."

"Someday Father with our education, Sarah and I will make a good living, but right now we won't have much in a monetary way to begin our life together. Still, what we'll both have is what we both love—these precious children and each other. We'll make due."

"You two," Father Jeff commented, "will do beautiful together. I couldn't be happier for the two of you."

"Tell me Sarah," Father Jeff asked, "what's your dream for a nice wedding?"

"I'd think friends, love ones, and family—maybe a simple white long wedding gown, white shoes, and a short veil. I definitely want my hair fixed in a nice ponytail since Ap mentioned that in his proposal. By the way Father, Ap's proposal was simply sweet and beautiful."

"Well," Father Jeff answered, "I knew we raised a good boy."

Sarah continued, "We should have matching wedding rings. Ajani and Zenna can be our ring bearers. Gbandi and Sadie will stand next to Johnna and Rahl who'll be our maid-of-honor and best man. The two boys can usher the people close to us."

"Sarah," Appy asked. "Do you think Johnna will be able to make it to our wedding?"

Sarah answered, "We need to pick a date like spring break when she's off. I'll e-mail her right away so she can give us a date that's good with her. I want my sister at my wedding, Ap. She'd never forgive me."

"Of course," Appy answered, "I just hope she can make it—that's all."

Father Jeff suggested that he could talk with the priest in town to see what plans he could make to have the wedding there.

"Father," Sarah answered, "I'd rather have the wedding outside at Sisters of Amity. We could decorate a little—maybe rent a tent for shade. Make it a wedding where all the people we care about can feel they're joining with us in our wedding ceremony."

"That sounds very nice, Sarah," Father Jeff said. "I'll talk with Father Reed about this, as well. I'm sure he'll agree that Sisters of Amity would make for a good place for the wedding celebration."

"Sarah and I both have some money saved. We'll make this work, but need to be frugal that's for sure."

"Appy," Father Jeff said. "I've put a few bucks away with your name on it just for such an occasion. I'll not take no for an answer."

Appy dropped his head with his hand cupped over his forehead, as his eyes were watery.

Sarah rubbed Appy's back and whispered, "Thank you, Father."

The dinner ended with dessert and coffee. All agreed that this was truly an eventful evening.

When Father Jeff and Appy arrived back at Sisters of Amity, Appy told Rahl about asking Sarah for her hand in marriage. That he wanted him to be his best man. Rahl was thrilled.

Appy continued, "Sarah wants to have the wedding here at Sisters of Amity outside under a tent."

"Oh," Rahl answered. "That'll be nice. Hey man, we could make a platform, paint it white, and adorn it with white flowers, something like a church sanctuary for Father Jeff and you to stand on." Rahl gripped Appy's shoulder and said, "We'll get this done."

"That's a terrific idea, Rahl."

"How soon is the wedding, Ap?"

"Well, Sarah wants Johnna to come in for the wedding, so she's contacting her by e-mail for a date around her schedule at school. Rahl, pray for our tolerance because Sarah and I are going to adopt Zenna, Ajani, Gbandi, and Sadie. We want to give them a life with parents."

"Well, I'm glad to hear Johnna will be coming in. However, Ap—that's a big family when just married. Of course, knowing you and Sarah, I'm sure you two can handle that many. I'll always be around to help you. You know, Ap, how much I love those kids. How much I'll miss the rest."

Appy replied, "I don't even want to think about that."

Sarah e-mailed Johnna back.

> Hi Johnna,
>
> Well, Ap proposed to me. He wants us to marry soon here in Africa. Of course, I want you to be my maid-of-honor. I wonder what'll be a good date for you. When is spring break? Get back with me soon. Flash—we are adopting Zenna, Ajani, Gbandi, and Sadie before Ap leaves for the States. I believe we'll take them out to eat to break the news. I also believe there'll be many tears, so I think "The Lanno House" will be the best place, even though, a bit expensive for the six of us. I'm trying to keep this short. E-mail me soon—like tonight. Love Sarah

Johnna e-mailed Sarah.

Sis,

Wow, how pleased I was when I got the news. My goodness you're going to be a mom of many. Its good, Ap, got a position in West Branch. I need to check out the school system there. Spring break is in three weeks around Easter. I'll look for a flight time and e-mail you. I, most likely, will want to come in a week ahead of time to help you get ready. In addition, I need to find a dress for myself that both of us like. Of course, I'll let mom and dad know. I'm so happy for you, Ap, and the children. Love you all. Johnna

CHAPTER 18

Rahl and Appy began to build the platform for the wedding ceremony. Sarah, on the other hand, was more interested in finding the right wedding gown. She shopped at the only American bridal shop in town for a simple white gown and wedding veil. After looking through two racks of gowns, she finally found the gown and veil that appealed to her.

The neckline of the gown appeared daintily scalloped just above her bosom. Below that on the gown's bodice were little flowers with a lavender touch in the center of each. Between each flower were iridescent sequins ornamenting the top half of the gown with seamed in eyelet cap sleeves that adorned the shoulders. The rest of the gown was full-length and form fitting to her body. She was also able to pick up a pair of white, goodly-wedged wedding shoes.

She felt confident in her choices. Her veil had to fit over her ponytail, so that took a great deal of thought on her part. She bought a lavender clamp with sparkles on it to hold her ponytail up.

"*Yes,*" she thought. "*I'm content with my choices.*"

She wished Ap could have helped her, but she also knew he wasn't supposed to see her in her wedding outfit. Nevertheless, she missed his input.

Appy e-mailed Sarah.

> Hi Sarah,
>
> We need to get a dinnertime set up where we'll be able to inform the children about our decision to adopt them and bring them to the States. What say you? Ap

Sarah e-mailed Ap.

> Hi Ap,
>
> I can go to dinner this coming Saturday night. How does that suit you, Dear? I feel very accomplished since I was able to purchase my gown, veil, and shoes. We need to shop for the children's outfits as soon as we break the news to them. I'm excited to witness and feel their reactions to the great news that we're going to spring upon them. I've goose bumps just thinking about it. Sarah

Ap e-mailed her back.

Hi Sweetheart,

Saturday sounds good. Yes, I too have goose bumps just thinking about what their precious reaction will be. Of course, our little African girl Zenna already thinks she belongs to us, but the rest of the children will be overwhelmed I'm sure. How much do I love you? Forever,

Dear, see you Saturday if all goes well with you. Ap

Appy told Gbandi, Sadie, and Ajani about dinner at "The Lanno House" Saturday night. Of course, Appy would let Zenna know on Saturday. He'd get her ready.

That evening everyone got into Appy's car (stuffed in) in his/her best attire. Appy headed for town. Rahl now living back at the mission house wanted to be with them at the restaurant to witness the uniqueness of this occasion first hand. Rahl felt that this was a beautiful humane story of his friends Sarah, Ap, and the children that all could love.

When seated in the restaurant, Zenna sat next to Appy on one side, Sarah on the other side. The rest sat at angles to each other on the large round table. Appy stood up and went to talk with the server who he informed of what was going on. He wanted to know if he could have pop served in champagne glasses for the children to toast this momentous occasion. Even the server was excited. She did all she could to promote their privacy. Rahl ordered wine. Sarah and Appy ordered the same. As the server brought drinks, Appy began to tell the children how much he and Sarah loved them—that neither could go back to the States without them. At this point, eyes began to pop at the news. Appy and Sarah held hands as Appy told the children that Sarah and he would like to adopt all four of them, and want to bring them back to the States as their very own children.

The children's mouths began to drop. They were seriously listening now.

Appy calmly said, "Ajani, Sarah and I want to be your mother and father. We don't ask that you forget your biological parents. We just want to love you the same way they did."

"What does biological parents' mean?" Ajani tearfully asked.

Sarah took over, "It only means Ajani—would you like to love us in the same manner you loved your mom and dad—because we want to love you like that and be your mom and dad forever."

Ajani cupped his hand over his mouth. He stood up, came around the table, put his hat on Sarah's head, and hugged Appy.

"I love you both. I'm so excited—that's why I'm crying."

Appy continued, "Gbandi and Sadie the same goes for you two. What do you think about all of this?"

"You know how I feel about you two," Gbandi said, "how loving of you to touch our hearts and lives in this manner. My parents, I can assure you, would love knowing about this. As ill as they were, they worried so much about my future."

"How about you, Sadie, would you like us to be your parents?" Appy asked.

Sadie overwhelmed by the news; put her head down on her folded arms crying loudly. Appy and Sarah went immediately to comfort her.

"Well, Sadie," Appy whispered, "Don't be shy my sweet talented teen." In addition, while Appy was hugging her, he asked her again. "Do you want us to be your mother and father?"

"Of course, I'm just stunned," she said through her tears. "It's the first time I've felt so loved in a longtime."

Sarah, Appy, and Rahl were tearing up at Sadie's statement.

"How about you Zenna—do you want me to be your daddy and Sarah your Momma?"

"Yep, Momma and Pap Pee Daddy," Zenna answered.

Rahl along with the rest, chuckled through tears at Zenna's newly invented name for Appy. It made complete sense to everyone that she couldn't give up the name Pap Pee that easily.

"Is, Zenna, Funny?"

"Yes, but you're the cutest funny girl." Appy said.

Rahl asked everyone to raise their fluted glasses in a toast to the new family that would unit with each other through love and law.

"Children," Sarah said, "Ap and I will be getting married in two weeks. Once the legal adoptions take place, your father will take you home to the States with him. I'll follow in six months. We'll then be a family, forever."

Sadie kept saying, "I can't believe this."

Appy answered her, "Father Jeff would say...BELIEVE!"

Ajani asked, "Will we all be sisters and brothers when we're adopted?"

Appy answered, "Good question, Ajani. You'll all be siblings, which means sisters and brothers. Sarah and I will be your legal mother and father. At that time, you may call us mom and dad if you like."

"I like," Ajani said.

"I like," Gbandi said.

"I like," Sadie said.

Zenna not quite sure what this was all about, "Me, too."

"Oh Zenna," Ajani said. "I sure like the idea of being your big brother."

"What about Beef—Pap Pee daddy?" Zenna was worried about her pet.

"Yes," Appy answered. "Biff, is also part of this family, as well. He'll live with us in our new home, Zenna."

"I love Beef."

"Say Biff," Appy instructed.

"Nope…Beef," Zenna answered.

Ajani, Gbandi, and Sadie began to do that musical clapping that always puzzled Appy.

Appy asked, "What does that musical clapping mean, kids?"

Gbandi answered, "It's a traditional African hand clapping that means something like—love those who love you."

Tears surfaced in Appy's eyes because that meant so much to him. It was how his teams of children felt about him—a secret code between all the children.

When Appy dropped Sarah off at her intern residence, he said, "Wow, Sarah who'll be able to sleep tonight?"

Sarah replied, "Not me for sure, I'll be going over everything said, how about you?"

"Oh yes," Appy answered. "Sleep won't come easily. I know from experience that the children won't sleep either—Zenna maybe."

"Yep, Pap Pee Daddy, while I'm thinking of Zenna, I need to have you bring the girls in town soon, so we can shop on my lunch hour for their wedding outfits."

Appy suggested, "How about we shop next Saturday when we'll have all day to find both the girl's and boy's outfits?"

"That sounds better yet, Ap. We can do that."

They kissed and agreed that they'd never forget this evening.

The following Saturday Appy, Sarah, and the children went into town. Each picked out their wedding outfits. Appy and Sarah also ordered the tent, flowers, and a nosegay for Sarah to hold. Sunday would also be a busy day since Johnna would arrive in Africa. She'd need transporting from the airport to the town.

Johnna came into Nairi's airport early in the morning around 6:00 a.m. Nairi's time. Sarah and Appy waited for passengers to come down the ramp of Air National. Soon Johnna exited the ramp. Sarah could see her mother and father right behind her. She was surprised and thrilled that they were able to come to Africa—that her father could give her away at her wedding.

"Ap, meet my parents Emily and Burt Henderson."

"Hello, Mother and Dad—I am so glad to meet you both. I hope you don't mind if I call you Mother and Dad. I've never had parents, so I like the idea of Sarah's parents being mine, too."

Burt answered, "Oh, that's fine with us, son. We never had a son." He chuckled.

Appy slid to the side to greet and hug Johnna. Thanked her for bringing the whole family to Africa to witness their marriage. Appy just happened to glance back at the arrival ramp. He thought someone looked a whole lot like, Sister Jenny.

"*No*," he thought, "*that makes no sense.*"

He did a second take.

"My gosh, Sarah, it's Sister Jenny."

He grabbed Sarah's hand. The two moved quickly toward her. Appy hugged her and lifted her off her feet. He whirled her around.

"Oh wow, Sister Jenny, I've missed you so much!"

He put her down. She moved to hug, Sarah.

"This is wonderful!" Appy chuckled with happiness. "Did you come with the Hendersons, Sister?"

"Yes, they were so good at arranging the flight that Father Jeff insisted on."

"Oh leave it to Father Jeff. He's so wonderful!"

Johnna hugged Sarah, "How about this for a surprise, Sis?"

"It's so great, Johnna! You're not only my sister, but also my best friend." The two hugged again.

Appy came close to Sarah. "Sarah, this completes the guest list on both sides."

"Yes, I know. It's the best!"

"What arrangements has Father Jeff made for you, Sister?" Appy asked.

"I believe I'm going to Sisters of Amity to spend the week with you and the children on a rollaway bed that Father Jeff has rented for me. Johnna and her parents are going to stay at the mission with, Rahl."

"These are workable plans, but you'll sleep on my bed, Sister. I'll take the rollaway bed."

"Well, Appy, we want you to be well rested for your wedding day."

"No need to worry about me, Sister Jenny. I'll be just fine. I insist."

"Ap," Burt mentioned. "I need to rent a car for the week we'll be here."

Appy chuckled, "That's a good idea since my car will never fit this many people in it." Sarah had to sit on her dad's lap to drive to the car rental garage behind the airport. Once there, Sister Jenny stayed in Appy's car with him and Sarah. Johnna and her parents set out for the mission house to meet with Rahl in the rental car.

They all agreed that they'd get together tomorrow at Sisters of Amity to discuss the wedding over lunch. Upon reaching Sisters of Amity, Sister Jenny could see Gbandi, Sadie, Ajani and Zenna dressed in their best attire waiting at the outside entrance to meet her. Of course, Father Jeff was all smiles.

Appy approached him; put his arm around him, "I was in shock when I saw her. This means so much to me."

"I thought it might, Appy."

Sister Jenny walked over to Father Jeff, "Well, we pulled it off."

Father Jeff put his arm around her shoulder. "Yes, it's so good to see you here."

"It's great to be here at this important time in Appy's life."

Father Jeff responded, "It's wonderful, Sister."

"Appy," Sister Jenny asked. "Will you two introduce me to your beloved children?"

They didn't need to because Zenna said, "Hi Sister Jenny, this is my brother Ajani," who was holding her hand, "and my doggie, Beef."

"Let me kiss you both on your foreheads." Sister Jenny requested.

Appy whispered to Sarah, "I'm jealous." Both chuckled.

She then moved toward Gbandi and Sadie—held Gbandi's hand with both her hands, then Sadie's hand with both her hands saying, "I'm so happy to finally meet you both. I've heard so much about you two. I, of course, know you both play baseball. I'm so anxious to watch a game and meet all the other players. To have you both coming to the United States to live close to us at St. Matthew is absolutely wonderful for Father Jeff and me."

Zenna wrapped her arms around Sister Jenny's waist. Moreover, while regarding Sister Jenny closely, she stated, "I'm going to live there too with Pap Pee Daddy and Momma Sarah when she comes."

"Oh yes," Sister Jenny answered. "You, Ajani, and Biff will also be there with Pap Pee daddy, Father Jeff, and I." She gently played with Zenna's hair, which looked much like two short ponytails, tightly curled, on top of her head—that bounced with her every movement.

"Sister Jenny," Appy quietly brought to her attention. "At four-an-a-half, Zenna wants to be sure she's included in any plans that Sarah and I have."

"Certainly," Sister Jenny replied. "I'll be sure to mention all four names when bringing this up again." She chuckled. "She's so sweet!"

Father Jeff nodded, "Everyone here finds her quite special."

Appy whispered to Sarah, "Did you hear your new name?"

"Yes dear, I'm so thrilled."

Father Jeff said, "Come in, we'll introduce Sister Jenny to Father Reed and have some cake and coffee."

"Yum, cake, Zenna," Ajani grabbed her hand. The group went inside.

Lately, the two seemed glued to each other. After all, Zenna was soon to be Ajani's sister. How could anyone make fun of that? Father Reed had been in the kitchen instructing the cooks on the luncheon menu. He moved toward the gathering room just as Sister Jenny along with Appy, Sarah, and the children entered.

"Sister Jenny," Father Jeff said. "This is Father Reed who has been dear to Appy and me for the last two plus years."

"I'm so happy to meet you, Father Reed. Both Appy and Father Jeff have a great deal of admiration for you."

"I admire them, as well," Father Reed, answered. "Come sit at our table and enjoy the cake the cooks have baked especially for you."

The cake read—Welcome, Sister Jenny.

Father Reed continued, "Sadie frosted the cake and wrote the message."

Appy put his arm around her, "Sadie, my sweet Sadie, you make me proud."

Sadie answered, "Gbandi set the table and put the napkins out, so he too was a big help."

Appy shook Gbandi's hand and thanked him. The two, so close in age, seemed to compliment each other in caring for Zenna and Ajani. Helping Appy and Sarah in anyway, they could. Sister Jenny, Father Jeff, and Appy talked and talked about the happenings at St. Matthew. The children listened intently about the place they'd be living at before purchasing their own home. Sister Jenny had many pictures to show the children.

Sadie being curious pointed and asked, "What's this in this room?"

Sister answered, "That's a sink for water and a tub to take a bath in. We call it a bathroom. The water comes out of the spigot filling the sink or tub with water. You can either wash your hands in the sink or sit in the tub and soak in the water."

"What do you think of that, Gbandi?" Sadie asked.

"I think we're going to be spoiled living in America." Gbandi answered.

Ajani said, "Sounds totally great to me."

"Me too, great," Zenna repeated after Ajani.

Later that day Appy e-mailed Rahl.

> Rahl, my good friend,
>
> How did you keep this so quiet from me? What a surprise. We've been talking all day about everything and anything. Of course, we have to fit in a baseball game for our guests. Sister Jenny wants to see a game. She so deserves to enjoy one. You'll meet her tomorrow at lunch. I know the girls want to shop for dresses for the wedding, so we'll plan around their shopping trips. We could meet them in town for lunch since we need to choose the tuxedo we want, size up, and order for the big day. I'm supposed to be nervous about getting married. I'm not! I'm so in love with my family and wife to be. My sadness will surface when Sarah and I are apart for six months. I'll have a first hand

experience of the suffering you went through, Rahl. Ap

Rahl e-mailed Appy.

Hi Sport,

No need to think that way, Ap, I'll be there with you on the weekends. We'll probably be busy getting you and the children set up in a home and school. I bet you were thrilled to see and be with, Sister Jenny. Johnna and I are going in town sometime this week for lunch and coffee, alone. It's something we promised each other upon meeting again—how about that, things are looking up for me, so no more negativity. Rahl

The next day everyone was up early getting themselves ready for the day ahead of them. Appy said, "Good morning, Sister Jenny. It's good to see you at our table."

Zenna entered the room, so as not to miss eating breakfast with Appy. She sat on his lap to wake up a bit more.

Sister Jenny regarding the two of them said, "I'm so happy for you, Sarah, and the children. When you left for Africa, I could see that you were a little afraid to face the outside world, but it seems like that feeling is past you now."

"Well Sister, I've been very lucky with Rahl, Sarah, and the children entering my life. I'm certainly not going to be alone, am I? It seems I've come all this way to find my way. I just hope I'm busy the next six months so that time passes by very fast. I'm going to really miss, Sarah."

"Well, there's a nice little thrift shop in West Branch where we can shop for winter coats for all the children. We'll have much to do. I'll keep you busy on your days off. I wonder what the children will think of the weather changes."

"Hard to say, Sister, but I've been thinking about building a skating rink for them when we get settled in a home of our own. I hope I can afford skates."

"Oh, I'm sure we have many old skates at St. Matthew that'll work just fine."

Zenna spoke, "Sister Jenny, I like eating my Pap Pee Daddy's jelly toast."

"I see that young lady." Sister Jenny answered.

After the morning hours had passed, everyone helped dress the children and clean up the gathering room. Sister Jenny and Sister Myra worked well together. Each knew how to care for children that's for sure. The cooks were planning a meal with Father Reed since another four guests would join them from the mission house at noon for lunch.

Before going to Sisters of Amity, Johnna wanted to stop and see Brent, Kaela, Lamar, and toddler Nettie since she hadn't seen them yet.

"Rahl, shall we leave a little early."

"Sure, how about now," Rahl answered.

Johnna and Rahl went in Rahl's jeep; the Henderson's in their rented car. Even though it was difficult to share their joy due to the language barrier, Brent's family was definitely excited to see her. The hugs and knowledge that they were here for Appy's and Sarah's wedding made the greeting warm. Johnna talked to, Nettie. She gave her a baby doll. This time Johnna came prepared with toys that the children would be thrilled to have.

Nettie just looked at her, hugged the baby doll, *"merci."*

The Hendersons were finding the scene difficult to witness.

Johnna's mother said, "Johnna in the future, I'll send as much as I can to Brent to help the village people."

By the time they got to Sisters of Amity, everybody was ready to enjoy the company and luncheon. Appy immediately introduced Sister Jenny to Rahl.

Rahl barely squeaked out, "I'm so in awe of you, Sister, that I'm shaking."

Sister Jenny picked up his hand and again held it with both of her hands. Rahl began to feel warmed by her touch. He calmed down instantly.

"I've prayed many nights for you, Rahl. I feel as if I know you very well."

"Thank you, Sister. I'm healed because of everyone's prayers."

Sarah let them know that Dr. Reese and Dr. Sodi went to bat for her with Mr. Cronc; he gave her two days off before the wedding, and two days after. Of course, she'd need to make them up once Appy left for the States, but it'd give her a couple more evenings to be with her new husband before going back to work. "Once you're gone, Ap, I'd prefer to work harder than usual, anyway."

"I know what you mean, Sarah girl."

"Saturday being our wedding day," Sarah continued, "I was thinking of going shopping on the Thursday before Saturday since I have that day off. I know that doesn't give us much time, so I hope everyone can choose dresses that don't have to be altered in anyway."

"Well Sarah," Appy stated, "Rahl and I were going to shop on the same day as you girls—maybe meet up for lunch, but our tuxedos might need sizing. I need to e-mail the store to see what the deal is."

"Okay Ap, do that," Sarah answered.

"I'm okay with Thursday," Johnna declared.

"That'll be fine with me, too," Sister Jenny said agreeably.

"I brought a nice full length dress with me, Sarah," her mother said. "Maybe you can check it out to see what you think of it."

"Sure mom; however, it's not reasonable to think you have to match the wedding party. I think you and Sister Jenny should wear something you like that fits comfortably. Keep in mind that it's very hot here under a midday sun. I'm sure you'll appreciate a sun hat, as well."

"Ap, dear," Sarah whispered to him, "You need to work on your vows, as I'll work on mine."

"Okay," Appy answered, "I usually don't write anything down when it comes to speeches, so my vows will probably be spontaneous."

"Oh no, I'll be reading mine. You'll just easily speak beautiful words as usual." Sarah said, seeming to sound a little insecure.

"You worry too much Sarah," Appy said. "If I thought you had no love for me, I wouldn't be marrying you, girl. Be cool, we'll be fine. We should hope that everyone will have fun and enjoy our wedding day, as we should also, sweetheart!"

"Yeah, you're right, Dear." Sarah answered in a much calmer voice.

CHAPTER 19

The week passed quickly. On the morning of the wedding day, it rained cooling things down somewhat. Because of the rainfall, everyone's attention seemed drawn to a most beautiful rainbow that loomed over the large white tent that the workers had just erected. The color lavender was in the rainbow, a color not often seen in a rainbow arch. Sister Jenny thought that was a blessing upon the couple since Sarah chose that color to ornament her dress and Johnna's, as well.

"See that rainbow, Zenna," Appy said while pointing his finger to the sky.

"Yes, Pap Pee Daddy. It's beautiful."

Appy commented, "I'd like to pull it out of that vast sky and save it for, Momma Sarah."

"Can you do that, Pap Pee Daddy?"

Appy chuckled, "No sweetheart. I'm just doing some wishful thinking."

"Maybe you can take a picture, Pap Pee Daddy," Zenna said, trying very hard to please him.

Gbandi had already thought to do that and was taking a picture of the amazing rainbow. Gbandi showed Zenna and Appy the picture he captured.

"Very nice Gbandi," Appy stated. "Sarah will really appreciate that shot."

"Yes, Gbandi, it's a pretty picture," Zenna remarked.

"Thank you, Zenna."

Gbandi would be in charge of all the wedding pictures since Sarah and Appy were trying to save on that score. Sister Jenny's digital camera displayed the picture taken, so Gbandi could be sure all shots were good, or if he needed to delete it to take another. Once Appy and the children left for the States, Sarah would make a wedding album. She'd bring it home to America with her.

The area by the sizeable tent was very busy with workers opening folding chairs, which Father Reed acquired on loan from the church in town, placing of the platform that Rahl and Appy constructed, and decorating the platform with the flowers delivered by truck—all very much adding to the beauty of a wedding chapel look. The little chapel that Father Reed had was much too small for this occasion. Sadie and Sister Myra, of course, were helping to arrange the altar cloths and candles to adorn their chapel under the tent. The two would also lay the wedding cloth runner that Sarah and the children would walk down to meet Appy and Father Jeff at the center of the tent.

Just then, Sarah, Johnna, and the Hendersons pulled up at Sisters of Amity while Rahl would be bringing in Brent's family in his jeep. Everyone was surprised at how well everything was coming together. The girls brought their dresses in. Put them in Appy's room that Sister Jenny now inhabited. Burt placed Rahl's, Appy's, and his own tuxedo in Father Reed's room.

Appy, Sarah, Sister Jenny, and the children sat and talked awhile.

Gbandi said, "Look Sarah." He showed her the rainbow.

"Oh my," Sarah said. "That's simply amazing, Ap."

"Yes, Sister Jenny thinks that blessing came from above," Appy answered.

Sarah whispered to Gbandi, "Keep up the good work, son."

Gbandi, Sadie, and Zenna were very drawn to Sister Jenny. Ajani remained loyal to Sister Clare. He'd find it difficult to break with the closeness they enjoyed. Sister Jenny was aware of Ajani's dependency on her. Together the two Sisters would work with him. Sister Jenny had shared the same closeness with Appy, so she'd help ease his way with special tenderness.

The time was drawing close for the wedding ceremony. The girls went in to put their wedding garments on. Sadie and Zenna were dressed very lovely in long dresses and new white shoes. Sarah fixed their hair. She did a final inspection on them.

"You girls look beautiful," Sarah remarked. "The floral beige and white dresses against your brown skin make me look pale in comparison."

"Thank you, Momma Sarah," Zenna answered.

"Yes, thank you, Sarah," Sadie said. "I feel beautiful in this dress. The way you did my hair is super special."

Everyone gathered around to help Sarah pull her dress over her ponytail. The dress fit beautifully. Johnna, Emily, Sister Jenny and Sister Myra were also dressing in their wedding garments.

"Johnna," Sarah mentioned. "We lucked out on your gown. The lavender is the exact same shade as the little flowers on my gown."

Johnna's gown was full length, made of lavender organdy, and had a sequin bodice.

"Yes, this gown is also very comfortable," Johnna, added. "These sleeves have a triangular shape above the elbows. They're nice and loose for any breeze that might happen along today."

Everyone looked beautiful and ready for the ceremony. The girls would stay in Appy's room until the wedding ceremony started.

Appy was in charge of Ajani and Gbandi in Father Reed's room. The men took turns using the room to dress in and then met out in the gathering area. Sarah had previously warned Appy not to pick up a baby for fear of a spit up. He definitely would pay attention to that detail on this day. The cooks, Jayla, and three others would stand by attending to the babies and toddlers.

The time had arrived. Everyone sat quietly under the tent. Father Jeff headed the procession. Appy and Rahl followed. Both stood next to each other on the lower step of the platform. To everyone's surprise, Ajani played his drum softly. Sadie sang wedding songs. She also sang other appropriate responses in the wedding mass, accompanied by Sister Clare on the piano. Sarah and Appy were so proud.

Sarah's father walked her down the aisle to Appy. He turned her over to him saying, "I ask you to be good to my daughter."

"Yes sir," Appy Answered. "You can depend on me to do just that."

Johnna carefully lifted Sarah's veil, so as not to disturb her hair. Gbandi and Zenna were right behind Sarah's father and came closer to Sarah and Appy.

Appy adorningly looked at Sarah and whispered, "You look gorgeous, girl."

Sarah whispered back, "You look handsome yourself, Ap."

Zenna whispered, "Shhhhh—only Father Jeff is supposed to talk."

Father Jeff winked at her and said, "She knows her stuff."

Appy cupped his mouth in a gesture to acknowledge what Zenna suggested.

<♣>

Father Jeff began:

"Since it's your intention to enter into marriage, join your hands, and declare your consent before God and His church."

"Appy do you take Sarah to be your wife? Do you promise to be true to her in good times and in bad, in sickness and in health, to love her and honor her all the days of your life?"

"I do," Appy, answered.

"Sarah do you take Appy to be your husband? Do you promise to be true to him in good times and in bad, in sickness and in health, to love him and honor him all the days of your life?"

"I do," Sarah, answered.

Father Jeff raised his head and said, "What God has joined, men must not divide."

Gbandi and Zenna handed Father Jeff wedding rings on little white pillows for a special blessing.

Appy placed a wedding ring on Sarah's ring finger: "Sarah take this ring as a sign of my love and fidelity—in the name of the Father, and the Son, and of the Holy Spirit."

Sarah also placed a wedding ring on Appy's ring finger: "Appy, take this ring as a sign of my love and fidelity—in the name of the Father, and the Son, and of the Holy Spirit."

Father Jeff pronounced them husband and wife. "Go, and be happy. Delight in the challenge ahead of you. You may kiss your bride, Appy."

Father Jeff had a tear streaming down his cheek. At that moment, luckily, he was able to turn the couple to face the people. Everyone began clapping with approval. Since the children also had tears in their eyes, Appy and Sarah took a moment to comfort them. The married couple then moved out into the crowd to greet family and friends. Zenna took Appy's hand greeting everyone, as well. She gently held a guest's arm; asked each for his/her name, then would say sweetly, "We're glad you're with us today." The guests thought that amazing for someone that young. Sadie and Ajani did a wonderful job with the music along with Sister Clare's piano. Gbandi was still busy snapping pictures at the reception. Many friends from the hospital came. Of course, Dr. Reese, Dr. Sodi, Mr. Cronc and his wife, Bill from the sporting good shop, and his friend Ari all came to witness the couple's wedding. With all the Sisters, Fathers, friends, and children from Sisters of Amity, it made for a sizeable wedding celebration for the couple.

Rahl was to give the wedding toast at the reception. He'd also allow the couple to say personal wedding vows that each had composed for the other.

"Sarah,

In my wildest imagination, I couldn't have guessed that the love of my life was halfway around the world in Africa. I believe God had something to do with this plan, girl. Not only will you be the wife I'll always love, but the mother of these wonderful children we have chosen together to share our life with. I've no problem committing my life to you and ours. Sarah I love you. I promise to tell you that until the day I die."

"Ap,

Your words to me have always been so beautiful. I wish I could use Gbandi's words and just say 'ditto' but that'd be far too easy. Needless-to-say, I thought it strange that two Americans approximately the same age would meet in Africa and find each other irresistible. I'd also like to thank the Lord for His plan for the two of us, and the abundance of love given us for children to be. It's my hope that many more children will join us. I'll respond to the love you show me, Ap, with love. I'll return respect shown me, with respect. I'll love you Appy Olsen until the end of my days."

The Sisters of Amity children just loved the desserts and wedding cake, and the reception fun that ensued. Everyone had to pitch in to help with the children.

Sister Myra said, "I've lost my favorite source of assistance today."

"I know," Appy, answered. "I don't feel right just walking around enjoying myself."

He glanced at Sarah, "But my lovely wife said she didn't want any spit up on me on our wedding day."

"I can't blame her there," Sister Myra commented.

"My wife," Sarah remarked. "I like the sound of that, Dear."

Sarah and Appy would leave soon to have a two-day honeymoon in town. Both had to be back to see Sister Jenny, Johnna, and the Hendersons take off at the airport for the States. Knowing that Ap only had two weeks remaining in Africa, Rahl once again was going to move into Sisters of Amity. That'd give Sarah, Ap, and children time together at the mission house to work on the adoption process.

He also thought it'd be good for them to be acquainted with each other in a homelike atmosphere.

When Sarah and Appy left for town, the party continued. Johnna and Rahl were dancing, laughing, and having a great time. Everyone enjoyed Sister Clare's, Sadie's, and Ajani's music often mentioning how well the group sounded. Appy and Sarah placed Sister Jenny and Father Jeff in charge of Zenna, Ajani, and Biff for the next couple of days. Gbandi and Sadie were old enough to care for themselves and each other. Of course, both would help with the young ones if need be.

While Johnna and Rahl were dancing, Rahl whispered in Johnna's ear, "I always had a glint in my eye for you Johnna, but I respected you enough not to make a move on you. I wasn't sure if I was just lonely enough to get into a relationship before my grieving was over which seemed selfish of me and disrespectful to you and Ruthy, so I gave myself time to be sure all intentions were good and right."

"Well Rahl, I wouldn't have allowed that to happen anyway since I'm well aware of the grieving process. It can plays tricks on you. I knew you needed time. It's hard to be whole when you suffer a loss like that. The loneliness caused from a loss like you experienced is devastating and frightening to many companions and spouses. Even when their love ones are suffering a terminal illness, and need to leave this world in peace with their consent, most find it very hard to make that decision."

"Johnna things are good, now. I'm asking you to be my steady girl when I come home. Would you wear my baseball cap—that seemingly worked for Appy and Sarah?"

Johnna chuckled, "We should find something we can call our own. It'll happen should we get together, I assure you."

"I still think I'll always be protective of my girl in the future because of what I experienced," Rahl said. "But that'll only be because I found a new love and couldn't bear going through what happened to me over a year ago. In the meantime, Johnna, we can communicate by e-mail if you like. I'll be in Saginaw in two weeks where I'll be able to phone you."

Rahl was rambling on since he was a little nervous with his proposals and Johnna's reaction to them.

"I'm going on the plane with Appy and Father Jeff to give a hand with the number of children they're taking back to the States. I'm also doing well enough financially, Johnna, to fly into up state New York to be with you. I think we should court awhile before taking the next step. What do you think?"

"I think you should kiss me first, so I can see if I like your style." She laughed.

"One thing for sure, Johnna," Rahl countered, "we both have a bit of the comedian in our spirits."

He slowly looked into her eyes, drew near her lips, and warmly kissed her. She lifted one foot, felt weak in the knees, with goose bumps rising on her arms. She kissed him again since she found herself truly enjoying the closeness.

"I definitely will want to see you in up state New York," Johnna said in a soft voice. "I have many places to show you around town. We can hope that a serious relationship will develop from our time spent together. I'm also spending three summer months with Sarah, Appy, and the children, as well."

"I'll be there, too," Rahl, answered, "So the four of us will have some good times together. Appy and Sarah will be thrilled to hear about this. We should kiss romantically in front of them and watch their reactions."

"Oh Rahl," Johnna said. "You're nasty! But yes—we can do that!"

Rahl asked, "May I date you the next two days—that's, if your parents won't mind being alone while we go out to dinner—maybe take in a movie?"

"I doubt very much if their feelings would be hurt," Johnna said. "I'll be spending time with them on the airplane. I know they certainly would like to see me with a fellow—I favor." The wedding reception ended at about 8:00 p.m. and Rahl, Johnna, and the Hendersons went back to the mission house to play some cards.

Back in town, Sarah and Appy were enjoying their honeymoon eve. Sarah had chosen a full-length navy blue, silk gown with a white lacy collar that she looked simply elegant in. Appy came up behind her, smelled the lavender in her hair and whispered, "I love you Sarah." He lightly stroked her breasts and ran his hands slowly down over her hips, turned her around, and kissed her sweetly. Dimming the lights, the two experienced the oneness of their union.

The following morning the two went to "The Lanno House" for breakfast where everyone expressed their happiness for them. Sarah ate six fried dippy eggs, fried potatoes, with rye toast and coffee.

Appy remarked, "Sarah you're eating like you have no energy left."

She blushed, "Well?"

In the two days, they have alone, it was important to discuss their roles as mother and father to four children.

"I know," Appy said. "There are some things best for you to handle with the girls and some things best for me to handle with the guys."

"Oh sure," Sarah replied. "But in the beginning when I'm absent, we'll ask Sister Jenny to handle any difficult problems with the girls.

It was so good of Rahl to offer us the mission house; even though, the commute will be longer for me."

"Well Dear," Appy answered, "Sadie, Gbandi, and I will do our share to have dinner ready, so that you can just relax after we eat. That way we can talk about things to come. Sarah, sweetheart, I feel as if I am *living out a dream* that has developed in my imagination for a very long time."

Sarah replied, "Together Ap we're going to make your dream a reality."

"Oh Sarah," Appy said. "I truly didn't go wrong when I picked you to love."

The two days passed fast for the honeymoon couple. Appy, Sarah, and Rahl would drive to the airport in Appy's car so their guests could board the plane for the States—Johnna with her parents and Sister Jenny in the leased car. As they gathered outside of Sisters of Amity to put the luggage in the cars, Rahl grabbed Johnna. He began to kiss her romantically.

"Rahl," Appy said totally in shock. "What's going on here?"

"A whole lot," Rahl answered. "Johnna and I are going to be an item in the future."

Appy chuckled, "Oh…my goodness! Sarah, did you hear that?"

Sarah giggled, "Sis, what have you two been up to? This is great news!"

Father Jeff would remain at Sisters of Amity. He shook hands with Sister Jenny letting her know that he and Appy would be seeing her again shortly and for her to get everything ready for about thirteen children.

Putting everyone on the plane for the States wasn't easy on anyone. Appy insisted that the Hendersons come to visit with Sarah and him. He assured them their chosen home would accommodate many—never to worry about putting them out. He enjoyed a large family.

"Johnna," Appy mentioned. "Of course, you know we expect you in the summer. Who knows, one of these summers you two might get married and live in our area—that'd be nice?"

Sister Jenny knew she'd see Appy in two weeks. She kissed Sarah on the cheek.

"I'll help Appy as much as I can in your absence," Sister said to Sarah.

"Oh, that's so loving of you," Sarah answered.

All three, Rahl, Appy, and Sarah watched as the plane entered the air.

Rahl turned to Appy, "How was the honeymoon?" All of a sudden, Rahl felt embarrassed as if maybe he didn't phrase that right in Sarah's presence. "Damn, I mean did you enjoy your honeymoon? I mean, well…you two know what I mean."

"Yes, Rahl—but the honeymoon just wasn't long enough," Appy, replied. "We'll need to repeat a honeymoon in the future when maybe you and Johnna will watch the children."

Rahl requested of Appy that he and Father Jeff consider taking Ukita back to the States—that both Johnna and him liked her and would have a greater chance of seeing her at St. Matthew.

"Of course," Appy said to Rahl. "I'll see to it."

The two weeks stay in the mission house was fun for everyone. Appy would drive the children back to Sisters of Amity for school and baseball games where Rahl helped him as usual. He'd pick up and drop Lamar off at the village after games. He was regretting much about leaving Lamar and his family in Africa. After games, the family headed home to greet Sarah when she came home from work. The adoption papers were about to be signed. The couple paid some up front monies and wrote up a payment schedule that'd help to support Sisters of Amity over a five-year period. Father Reed arranged this agreement with the couple because he was so grateful for the life the two would give these four children, while helping out the others left behind.

Appy let Father Reed know—that this wasn't nearly good enough.

"Father Reed, I'm having a hard time leaving here without every one of them."

Father Reed put his arm around Appy, "We do what we can, Appy."

Back at the mission house, Appy and Sarah could see a change in the children in their new environment. It'd be hard to describe, but it appeared like confidence in their future existence. Sadie loved singing while cleaning the mission house. Gbandi and Appy still repaired computers for the hospital and others. Everyone knew the time had come for the group to leave, so if they wanted their computer fixed, now was the time. Consequently, the two were very busy.

Appy let Gbandi drive while he sat in the passenger seat to Sisters of Amity, so that the children could attend school. When they arrive in the States, Appy thought that both Gbandi and Sadie would want a driver's license. He once thought that exciting. It was a big thing when Appy learned to drive. He naturally thought that Sadie and Gbandi would feel the same thrill.

"Sarah, you know, Gbandi feels like a big shot driving the car, but Sadie seems to prefer cleaning, making beds, and cooking. She seems happiest doing these kinds of chores."

"That's not all bad," Sarah remarked. "Some girls are natural homemakers. I have a feeling these two will be good teens, Ap, mainly because they've had many hardships already. I'm sure they'll appreciate family. Still, we'll need to keep them involved with good peer groups."

"For sure," Appy answered.

Ajani, Zenna, and Biff played endlessly. These two were thrilled with their new home life in which they viewed mom and dad their heroes. Sadie gave them the job of setting the table for breakfast and dinner. The two thought they worked too hard, so they played the rest of the day when out of school or not at games. Sometimes Ajani played his drum while Zenna danced around.

Appy laughed at them. He said to Sarah, "We have a singer, a drummer, a dancer, and a computer apprentice. How unique is that, girl!"

CHAPTER 20

A week before leaving for the States; the two priests, Appy, and Rahl came together for breakfast at Sisters of Amity to discuss their departure, and the children that were to make the trip to the States with them; namely, Gbandi, Ajani, Zenna, Sadie, Ukita, Jabarl, Jimi, Tobi, three babies, Jayla and Tanesha. Having friends make the trip together assured the children that they could handle the change. A chartered plane would take them to Amsterdam, then into Michigan via another airliner. From there a school bus would pick them up at the airport to transport them to St. Matthew. Gbandi and Sadie would be a big help holding the babies. Appy, Rahl, and Father Jeff would supervise and care for the rest.

Appy also wanted to get together with Mr. Cronc and Bill to see if they could carry on with the baseball teams. Lamar's village children would need training to make up the number needed to play, but Lamar knew the baseball rules. All the equipment would remain. Lamar had practiced with some of the children at the village, so Appy knew there was an interest in playing the game. Lamar had also learned English well enough to carry on the games with English speaking Mr. Cronc and Bill. He could interpret messages to those who only spoke French. As other orphan homes come into Africa to bring Sisters of Amity's children to other parts of the world for adoption in loving families, these baseball games may take place only at the French village where Lamar could help the children enjoy the game. Appy would write-up papers asking that all baseball equipment go to the village people once Sisters of Amity closed. Appy was also extremely aware that if there were further uprisings in the area, Sisters of Amity might never close.

Appy, Rahl, Father Jeff, and all the children were packing for their journey home. Everyone seemed excited except for Appy who knew this was definitely bittersweet. Sarah wouldn't be able to see her husband or children off for the States since she had to work to make up the time she took off for their wedding. The night before the two made a solemn promise to work hard to ward off the loneliness and e-mail each other everyday. They'd put all their money together to promote the children's welfare—a home, school clothing and supplies, and all expenses involved in everyday living.

Appy had the responsibility of handling the children once arriving in the States. Sarah was to apply herself to her internship, help Appy via e-mail with organization that could only help him, and love the children from a distance. The day of the flight Father Jeff, Appy, and Rahl said their good-byes to the wonderful people they had grown so close to, especially Father Reed, Sister Myra, Sister Clare, and the cooks of Sisters of Amity who were as dear to them as anyone else.

At the airport, it was a humorous scene; whereby, the three men looked like mother ducks with their ducklings following them on the airplane ramp. Even the men laughed at themselves and had Gbandi and Sadie laughing, too. Father Jeff, Appy, and Rahl each had a baby in a backpack strapped to them to enable their hands to be free to handle other children.

Once inside the airplane and the children were seated—all let out a big sigh.

Zenna said to the pilot, "This is like a big bird."

"You're right honey," the pilot answered, "A big steel bird." He chuckled.

For almost the whole flight, Zenna and Ajani sat together. Ukita and Jabarl sat on the other side of the aisle. They had a great time together. Father Jeff was feeding a baby by bottle, Appy putting one baby to sleep by rocking him in his arms, and Rahl had a baby that decided she wanted to cry herself to sleep. Sadie took the baby from, Rahl. She walked her in the aisle singing softly to her until she fell asleep and then placed her back in Rahl's arms.

Rahl said, "Thanks Sadie, I need to learn how to sing."

"Damn," Rahl said to Appy. "I'm not sure I'd be good with a newborn. That crying makes me feel helpless."

Appy answered, "Just keep walking and rocking them I guess. Look at Sadie—she's the greatest. You'd come to know your own baby just like Sadie understands what that little baby in your lap needed."

Coming into Metro airport, Appy said, "Hey kids you're officially in the United States of America!"

Father Jeff said to Appy and Rahl, "It's good to be back."

Once off the plane, Sister Jenny, who came along on the bus to greet and welcome everyone home, was a big help with boarding the children on the bus. She asked all the children to whisper since there was no sound barrier in the bus and three babies were asleep. The children did what she asked because they knew she was good at handing out treats. Sure enough, she passed out a big sucker to each. Even the older ones enjoyed that.

Father Jeff said, "It's been a long time since I've been on a school bus."

"I know what you mean," Rahl answered.

Appy retorted, "I'm not too crazy about airplanes, but I must admit the flight was smooth all the way, and not nearly as bumpy on my rump as this bus, for sure."

Everyone laughed.

Sister Jenny remarked, "It's good to have you back in the States. We've done our best to make things pleasant for your return. Father Larry and Sister Eunice have outdone themselves to make accommodations nice for the babies and the older children, as well. The cooks have made cupcakes as a treat for the little ones."

"Little ones," Rahl quietly said, "Hell that sounds good to this big one."

"Me too, Sister," Appy whispered.

"There's enough for everyone," Sister said smiling.

Rahl would stay for two days at St. Matthew until Appy chose a car of his own to drive Rahl to Saginaw. The two looked for a car together, searching several dealerships, before Appy found the one he wanted. The children were going to attend school at St. Matthew, so Sister Jenny had already enrolled them. Father Jeff set Appy up with Tracy who had been a resident at St. Matthew. Once leaving the home, she had become a realtor. Father Jeff was always loyal to "his" children that once lived at St. Matthew's orphanage. Tracy told Appy she'd take him house hunting on the weekend.

Appy chose the car he wanted. He took Rahl to his father's home in Saginaw. It was good to meet Rahl's mother. Appy also enjoyed talking about his job with Rahl's father. Even though the day was very pleasant, Appy felt he couldn't stay away from the children for long. He headed home after a couple of hours.

A day later, Tracy took Appy to an old house on five acres. Appy looked with interest at this home with columns at the front entrance and a wrap around porch that seemed to need a few new floorboards.

"How many bedrooms are there?" Appy inquired.

"Six," Tracy said, "Four good-size bedrooms upstairs with a bath, two on the first floor."

Appy said, "It's large enough, but needs some repair. It reminds me of an unkempt White House, but on a smaller scale."

"Yes," Tracy answered. "It's been on the market a long time, so presumably it must have its faults. I can tell by the height of the weeds, grass, and overgrown shrubs."

"Yes," Appy commented. "Looks a little bit like a haunted White House."

Both chuckled.

"Follow me; we'll take a closer look, Appy."

"Sure Tracy—this I know, I'll have to cut the grass and clean things up before sending my wife any pictures of this place."

Tracy unlocked the door. The two entered. Appy could see some wall damage around a chimney. It looked to Appy as if the chimney needed some tuck-pointing.

"Apparently," Appy pointed out to Tracy, "there's a leak causing damage to the wall next to the chimney."

"Yes," Tracy, answered, "It appears to me that it could use a new roof."

"Tracy, I'd like to go upstairs to see how strong the staircase is. Okay, I'd say."

"Yes, not bad at all," Tracy replied.

"Well Tracy," Appy said, "I need to have the house inspected before purchasing, but I like the possibilities of this home. I believe I saw something that looked like a laundry room upstairs, which could be used as a seventh bedroom."

"How many children do you have?" Tracy asked, nicely.

"Four at this time, but I expect to have more. Tracy I'd like to get on this right away. The kitchen is huge."

"Yes," Tracy stated, "Its 33 feet long by 16 feet wide. The dining room is a good size, as well."

Appy made the comment, "The library could be turned into my office. It's not as large as I'd like, but it'll do for now. I'd definitely like to change the rounded arch openings going into each room to square openings in an attempt to modernize the home a bit. This house has great possibilities, but not without a lot of work. How many bathrooms did you say downstairs?"

"Two," Tracy said, "One is large enough for a first floor laundry—a washer and dryer would fit in there, nicely."

"I'd like to look at the basement, Tracy. Wow, a large storage space down here—that's good. Great Tracy, I like it. I'll put a bid on it, but there's no way I can pay the price they're asking with all the needed repairs. Go $20,000.00 less or ask the owner to put a new roof on and fix the chimney. We'll see what comes about."

"Okay Appy, we'll also write in the purchase agreement that the purchase price will be subject to change after inspection. If the inspector comes up with many more problems that we're unaware of, we can come down more or back out of the deal altogether. We can even ask the owner to do further repairs."

Appy was anxious to e-mail Sarah.

Hi Sarah,

I'm placing a bid on a big, old white home. I believe it needs a new roof and some drywall repairs inside. It'd look nice with squared-off entrances rather than arched ones. I'll need all the children to help me clean up the weedy yard. Inside the home, there's six plus bedrooms, huge kitchen, very large sitting room, dining room, library, and three bathrooms. Oh Sarah, the home also sits nicely on a five-acre parcel of land that's partially wooded. I'll send you pictures, but only if the bid is accepted, that is. I'm truly excited about this home. First things first, Sarah, the roof, furnace, and electrical connections will all need inspection to be sure this house has the potential of being a safe home for our family.

One month has passed. I'm on the countdown until you're with me again. The children miss you, especially, Zenna. We need you to send a video. That way she can see you and hear your voice. Once settled in our home, I'll be too busy to miss you... fat chance. I took Gbandi, Sadie, and Sister Jenny to see the house earlier today. Gbandi questioned, 'Dad, do you think we can handle the yard work by ourselves?' I told him that Rahl might come in to help us if we get this house. However, Sadie, the busy bee, is anxious to start washing floors and cleaning toilets. She's our biggest asset, Sarah. What a girl! Bless her heart; she's so thrilled with her new life. Had we left her behind, I couldn't have lived with myself. Our two girls and two sons make me cherish you more than you'll ever know. Please e-mail the children—that'll help me keep the family intact. Ap

Sarah thinking over what Appy said thought she'd e-mail, Sadie.

Hi Sadie,

Your daddy tells me that you're a diamond in the rough. Don't overwork yourself. I ache to be there with you to help. When at school, be sure to join choir. I understand Sister Jenny took you shopping for school clothes. She's such a dear. I am sending my love for now. E-mail me soon. Love Mom

Hi Zenna,

How's my little girl? Are you taking care of Biff? I hope so. Soon you'll have a nice big yard to run with him and watch him romp in fun. I hear you and Ajani help Sister Jenny with setting the table for breakfast. I wish I could be there when you start school for the first time. I also hear you have some nice new clothes and shoes. Do you and Ukita still dance to Ajani's drum and Sadie's beautiful singing? I love you sweet pea. Momma Sarah

CHAPTER 21

Tracy was able to get the home on Blossom Heath for Appy and Sarah. The closing was to take place in two weeks—leaving enough time for the owner to install a new roof on the home and repair the chimney. Appy also contracted with the home improvers to redo the arched openings—squaring them off.

Rahl was coming in on the weekend after the house closing. Appy, Gbandi, and Rahl would begin to hack away at the jungle around the home. To Appy, the new roof made it possible to see that this house would one day be presentable as a decent home.

When the weekend came, the men rented equipment to trim and cut away vines and bushes. Sadie and Zenna cleaned the bedrooms and bathrooms upstairs. Sadie let Zenna pick up junk that was lying around on all the floors while she swept the bedroom floors. She'd wash them if she had enough time after cleaning the bathrooms.

"I love this house, Zenna, do you?"

"Yes," Zenna said. "But I'll like school better. I miss Momma Sarah…."

Zenna told Sadie. "I need her to take me to school on my first day."

"Oh Zenna, you'll be fine until mom comes home," Sadie answered. "Sister Jenny will be sure to be with you."

"Yeah," Zenna said, "I love Pap Pee daddy a whole bunch and Biff and Ajani, but they can't take me to school either."

"How about me, do you love me?" Sadie asked.

"I love you, Gbandi, Father Jeff, Sister Jenny…and Rahl."

By the end of the day, on their journey back to St. Matthew everyone looked like they came out of a war zone. All day Appy and Rahl cut branches, shrubs, and vines while Gbandi and Ajani dragged the debris and made piles and piles of burning materials.

Ajani asked, "Dad, how much are you paying us for all this hard work?"

"Not one red cent," Appy said, "Because this is your home, too. Which means, son, we all must take care of it; although, Rahl and I might consider taking you to the zoo in the next couple of weeks."

"Oh wow," Ajani said with a big smile. "That sounds like something I'll like very much. Can Jabarl go with us?"

Appy answered. "We'll fit in as many as possible. What do you think, Rahl?"

Rahl answered, "Sure, sounds terrific to me. We could take two cars or maybe the driver of the school bus could take us."

"That's good thinking, Rahl. I'll check that out."

Appy, Rahl, Gbandi, and Ajani took a walk into the woodland area behind the house. They could see the beauty of the woods with its mossy trees and spindly branches that seemingly blocked off the sky's light from above.

Gbandi questioned, "Do we need to clean this area up, dad?"

"No," Appy and Rahl laughed.

"Can we build a fort out here, Dad?" Ajani asked.

"That's a possibility Ajani," his dad answered.

The following weekend Rahl and the boys helped Appy burn debris. The workers were there to install both the new electrical box and new furnace. Appy had brought a microwave oven to cook hot dogs once the electricity came back on.

After an hour or so, the electric returned. While eating Rahl mentioned, "My mother says she has bed frames and mattresses for you if you want them. She wants to make the large bedroom upstairs into a nice big library where she can have her computer, books, and writing desk. She needed a good reason to remove these furnishings. Your four children encouraged her to do it, now."

"Oh, wow, Rahl that's so kind of her! We need so much—the mattresses will cover a big expense. We'll definitely be able to move in sooner."

Rahl continued, "She said two twin beds and one double."

"The twin beds sound good for Gbandi and Ajani," Appy answered excitedly. "I think Sadie might like the double bed. Then...I'll only have to get a bed for Zenna, Sarah and me."

"If you like Appy, I'm selfish enough to want to buy you a couple of twin size beds, so that when Johnna and I come in town, we won't have to sleep in our bags on these damn hardwood floors. It isn't like the ground outside that gives a little."

"The one thing you're not is selfish, Rahl. That's so good of you." Appy said, "Yes, more than likely the floor is probably where you'd wind up since I can't master all our needs right off." He chuckled.

Rahl said, "You and Gbandi will need to come down with a small moving van to pick up the beds at my mother's house."

"Rahl," Appy stated, "I'll want to do that right away so that we'll be closer to a move in. Do you want to go shopping with me for those twin beds, Rahl?"

"Yeah," Rahl answered. "That'd be good to do together so that they can be delivered to the house. I'll need to make it next weekend because I'm flying into up state New York the following week."

"I'm jealous that you get to see your girl," Appy intentionally sounded like he was whining. "How's that going, anyway?"

"Very well," Rahl answered. "I'm damn anxious to see her that's for sure!"

Appy e-mailed Sarah that evening:

Hi Dear,

Zenna had her first day at school. Sister Jenny said the teacher asked Zenna if her mother and father would be coming, too. She said, 'No, my Momma Sarah and Pap Pee Daddy can't be here today. Sister Jenny will wait for me until school is over and take me back to Pap Pee Daddy and Biff, my dog.' When Zenna walked off to play with the children in the room, Sister Jenny spoke with the teacher soothing the way for an understanding between Zenna and her teacher, Mindy.

To catch you up sweetheart, Gbandi and Sadie are both in driver's training now. Father Larry is as good with them as he was with me as a boy. The practices in the parking lot also helped them to develop a relationship with him. Furthermore, Father Larry tells me they're doing well. I love you babe; I miss cuddling with you. Ap

Appy worked every weekday. He spent every evening at St. Matthew with the children. Appy hoped to settle in the new home on Blossom Heath soon, so he could pursue his Master's Degree. His work gave him one day a week to attend college during working hours. If need be, he could go an hour or two in the evening while Sadie and Gbandi watch Ajani and Zenna. He was well aware that more education would boost his paycheck. It could be a big help in raising the children. Maybe even make it possible to help the children through college. That day Appy received a letter from Chikae. It read.

Hi Ap,

I miss you a great deal and all the children at Sisters of Amity. I visited Father Reed. I see you took quite a few with you to the States. Father Reed got me in touch with Mr. Cronc at Cinnae Hospital. I've contracted with him to do the computer repairs. I'm so excited. He'll pay me enough so I can rent a room for the weekdays and go home on the weekends.

Mama and Papa say 'hello,' and to tell you again that they'll never forget you. Both my parents are praying that all goes well with your new family and with Rahl. I receive Gbandi's e-mail with cheer. I, of course, have my driver's license and work permit now. I've been attending a course in computer repair, but haven't learned as much as you taught me. If need be, I'll get in touch with you should I have any serious problems. I miss you, Sarah, and the rest of the team.

Team player, Chikae

Months had gone by and the winter was setting in. Appy had the bare necessities to make life comfortable for him and the children. Each child got a warm comforter for their birthday to match the newly painted bedrooms that Gbandi and Appy tackled themselves. Soon Sarah would be with them. She'd put the final touches on their home. That, of course, would be the best day for everyone. Appy was busy in his spare time. He made a skating rink by making snow borders, wetting and packing them down, laid a heavy plastic tarp over the whole space and added water on a cold day to make a fine ice rink.

It was amazing how good Zenna was on ice. Sister Jenny gave her a used pair of skates that fit her perfectly.

She told Sister Jenny, "I want to be a skater and dance on ice."

She also giggled and giggled when Ajani pulled her around the rink. Ajani put Biff on a plastic sled with Zenna and pushed them from one end of the rink to the other repeatedly. "This is as much fun as our trip to the zoo." Ajani said.

Appy thought to himself, "*This boy is very much like me. I adore him.* Ajani have you e-mailed your mom, lately?" Appy inquired.

Hi mom,

I'm in band now. My teacher says he's very proud of my ability to play the drums as good as any man, but that I need to learn to read notes. We'll be having a winter wonderland performance at school. My band teacher wants both Sadie and I to be in it. I told him about Sadie's voice. Sadie said, 'What did you do that for?' She's so shy, Mom. Did you know that? I told her that I've never been a shy drummer. She said, 'You're not me!' I said I hope not—I'm a boy.

I've been having great fun outside in the snow. Snow is something I've never seen before. It's cold stuff. Zenna and I play a lot out on the ice with, Biff. Dad brings Jabarl and Ukita over on the weekends to sleep and play with us. I miss you, Mom. Your son Ajani

Finally, a month later, Gbandi picked up his mother at the airport since Appy worked that day.

"Oh, at last," Sarah said. "It's so good to see you, and to be back in the States. Africa has some uprisings right now. I've worried so much about the people there. Gbandi, you now live in a great country. You should never forget that."

"You bet," Gbandi, answered.

Upon arriving at her new home on Blossom Heath, the children greeted her.

Zenna cried out, "I've missed your face Momma Sarah—so much."

Ajani kissed and hugged her. He put his hat on her head.

"That's so sweet of you, Ajani." as Sarah hugged and kissed him again.

After hugging her mother, Sadie took her to the master suite to put her things away. Sarah could see Appy's shirt hanging over a chair. She picked it up. While rubbing it against her cheek—she sighed.

After a while, Sadie called out, "Come on, Mom. I want to take you through your house."

"It looks like you have done such a good job cleaning, Sadie."

"Well, I went through it special for your homecoming."

Sarah put her arm around Sadie, "What would we do without you, sweetheart?"

"I could ask that same question, Mom," Sadie countered, "What I would do without you and dad?"

"Ah," Sarah sighed.

Just then Gbandi announced, "Dad said he'd be home around five o'clock this evening."

In the meantime, everyone sat down again and talked. Sadie served coffee with a piece of cake. Zenna brought her chair close, very close to her mom's chair. Everyone had a lot to say to catch up with the goings on; even though, Appy kept Sarah abreast of everything through his nightly e-mails. Just then, Biff came in. Sarah had to stand up to greet him for fear he was ready to jump in her lap.

"Biff," Sarah chuckled, "you still remember me. What a smart and loving dog you are."

She petted him until he calmed down, and then rejoined the children in conversation while Biff lay at her feet under the table. At five that evening, the home really came alive in a joyful coming together as Appy and Sarah were ecstatic to see and hold each other. Appy beside himself in happiness, shouted, "What a day this is!" He stared at Sarah, "Let me smell your hair to be sure you're here."

Sarah had a tear surface, "I'm here, dear. Finally…I'm here!"

As the weeks passed, Sarah brought her home together. She had a trust fund left to her by a great aunt who had no children, which enabled her to live in Africa. Now, she'd use some of it for a few pieces of furniture needed in her sitting room. Sister Jenny and Sarah also went to estate sales and store sales to find chest of drawers with mirrors for the children. This would be a big relief since most of the children's clothes were in cardboard boxes on the floor. She also found a nice dining room set and hutch with drawers to store her place mats and tablecloths in. These pieces were in excellent condition as if just purchased out of a store.

At one estate sale, she found a perfect area rug for under the dining room table, also one for the great room where the children could lie down on to watch television in the evening and enjoy popcorn. Since the room was very large, Appy and Sarah wanted to purchase comfortable overstuffed chairs, side end tables, and tables and chairs where the children could do their homework. However, it seemed they needed more time to save for it since Appy had just bought bikes for himself, Sarah, Ajani, and Zenna. They also needed to purchase a used car for Sadie and Gbandi to drive to school and back. For sure, every penny counted these days. Still, the family enjoyed Sarah's homey touches.

CHAPTER 22

Within ten years, Sarah and Appy had five more biological children...all boys, Jeffrey (after Father Jeff), Samuel, Gus, Gerard, and Edward. The older children were a big help getting the younger ones this far since there wasn't much of an age difference between the little ones. In addition, Rahl and Johnna were married. The couple had adopted Ukita and had two more, Elizabeth and Cody. Sarah and Johnna enjoyed their closeness. Appy and Rahl were like brothers, as well.

Appy often kept the neighborhood active in baseball games, skating, zoo trips, and picnics at his home. All the fathers joined in to help at the events allowing Appy and Rahl to have many friends in the community. Of Course, Father Jeff and Father Larry brought the children that were old enough from St. Matthew to join in the fun, have hot dogs and ice cream cones with Appy, Sarah, and family—and run the acres with Appy's two new dogs, Rowdy and Bess. Biff was now twelve years old. Moreover, Appy felt that he had a good long life, but that time was running out for him in this world—seeming slow and tired. Ladi, of course, was in doggie heaven by this time.

Sarah also had many close friendships with neighbor women. She often attended to their children when sick; and was involved at St Matthew in the woman's choir. She served as a good role model to Sadie who also volunteered her voice for many years at church.

By this time, Appy had his PhD, which afforded him a very good livelihood. Sarah worked at the hospital part-time as a pediatrician on staff. As for Rahl, he was doing well due to his promotion for his writings on Africa. Appy's family listened to the news every night on television to see Uncle Rahl reporting everyday news events. Johnna also had a full-time job teaching 12th grade in the district school system. She was lucky to have summers off to enjoy the family. Gbandi and Sadie both were twenty-four years old, Zenna 15 and Ajani 18.

At the breakfast table, Appy made the comment, "Sarah, it's hard to believe that Zenna is going to be in driver's training."

In privacy, Zenna still called her father Pap Pee Daddy, and her mother, Momma Sarah. She didn't want to change that at all, but her peers looked at her strange, so she controlled herself.

"I hope," Sarah, replied, "she'll be a good driver and be able to take the younger ones to St. Matthew's schoolhouse safely for us."

Appy continued, "It's also hard to believe that Gbandi is working with me and has his Bachelor's Degree. That Sadie has a Bachelor's

Degree in music paid for by her own winnings of years ago. Good for her to have used that money for what it was meant for."

"Yeah," Sarah responded. "I'm looking forward to the musical movie she's going to sing for. For sure, St. Matthew will miss her as lead singer in the choir when she leaves to make this musical movie recording."

Sadie was now engaged to marry a black man named Rob Adam right after her movie event was finished. She wanted an outside wedding like her parents, but at the home on Blossom Heath. Gbandi had yet to find a special girl of interest. Still, he dated frequently.

Appy thirty-five and Sarah thirty-six were now approaching the end of childbearing years. The two enjoyed having young ones around them, but felt that they were finished having children themselves. They'd wait on the many grandchildren hoped for from their nine children. Surely, Sadie and Gbandi would bring babies into their life soon, even though five of their biological children were still very young.

Later that day Father Reed e-mailed Appy and Sarah

Hi folks,

I think about you every day. I must say I enjoy the pictures I get of the children. Love to every one of you! I hear from Father Jeff via e-mail. Of course,

I respond in kind. Sarah's parents, the Hendersons, send clothes and toys to both the French village and Sisters of Amity. We've received these gifts for many years. We're so grateful. Lamar is a man now and remains devoted to the village children and baseball. He's one fine man. He says in many ways you were his mentor. He thinks highly of you and Rahl. I helped Chikae attain his job with Mr. Cronc—another man who you touched so deeply.

As Sarah can understand, things here in Nairi are getting rough again. It seems peace has no consistency in Africa. I've two boys, each fifteen years of age, and one thirteen year old girl here at Sisters of Amity—Iman, Paki, and Aza. All are African born children who've lost their parents in these uprisings. I am wondering if you might have a place in your heart and home to take these blossoming teens in. I fear the guerrilla army will come through here and take all children that can carry a rifle.

These children are between youth and adulthood. Five more years of stability will mean so much to them. For the most part, these militant men leave Sisters of Amity alone, but should they need the young to fight their war, they'll come looking. Please think this over. You won't hurt my feelings should this be too much of a burden on you two. The children are good youths coming from stable homes. Moreover, these teens should make new parents proud. Sincerely yours, Father Reed.

Later that day Appy said, "Sarah, I'd like to take you out to dinner tonight. I've something I need to talk to you about. We can go to Bridge Port Country Club and order that steak dinner that we both love so much."

"Yum," Sarah answered, "Sounds good to me."

That evening Sarah dressed up. Appy wore dress pants, as well.

"It feels good to have a date with you, Sarah," Appy winked at her. "With Gbandi as old as he is, we need to do this more often—what say you?"

"Yes, of course," Sarah answered. "But it's tough when there're so many mouths to feed at home. Like today, I made spaghetti for everyone's dinner, so the only thing I'm enjoying tonight is being alone with you." she chuckled.

"Yeah, you're right," Appy commented. "I've something to ask of you, which I think could be a little selfish after your last remark."

"What is it?" Sarah asked.

"Well, I got an e-mail from Father Reed today. He has two boys each fifteen years of age and a girl age thirteen that he'd like us to adopt and bring to the States. At this time, there are uprisings in Africa. He fears these warriors will take these three to fight for them."

"Oh no, Ap," Sarah looked disturbed, "How could grown men take these young innocents to fight a cause they know nothing about, putting their lives in jeopardy, allowing them to witness the horrors of war at thirteen and fifteen years of age?"

Appy answered, "I don't know, but it seems these uprisings are never ending in Africa with no sight of a strong peaceful government coming forward."

"We need to go home and talk to our family," Sarah said. "We have the means to bring them in and still do right by the children we now have, but we'll probably have to forget that European trip we were planning and saving for."

Appy continued, "It's like Father Reed said, these children need five years of stability, which will enable them to cross over into adulthood with fewer childhood scars."

The server took their order for steak dinners and each a glass of cranberry wine.

"Ap," Sarah said. "We need to watch for any reactions from our girl's Sadie and Zenna, so as not to create jealousy in our family.

I know they're special and wonderful, but they've received all the attention up to now."

"So true," Appy answered. "We need to make this decision together as a family, with joy in our hearts and minds for the newcomers, or not even consider doing this."

"Yes," Sarah responded. "We'll discuss this tomorrow since its Saturday and everyone should be home to take part in this decision."

"Okay," Appy answered.

"Sarah, after eleven years of marriage, you're still everything I need in my life. Thank you for this lovely evening out, and the smell of lavender around me."

"Oh Ap," Sarah sighed, "Thank you for being you!"

The next day after Saturday brunch, Appy brought up the subject about bringing Iman, Paki, and Aza into their home.

Appy questioned, "Do any of you have any concerns about sharing your family with these three?"

"Well dad," Gbandi said, "it's the same thing that Chikae went through, but he and Reva at least got their parents back. These uprisings are destroying families."

Appy didn't tell the children about Father Reed's fear.

Gbandi continued, "I'm confident in your love for me. These young people deserve a happy and wonderful life after what they've experienced. You two have given every one here an abundance of love. Yes, I can share that love with Iman, Paki, and Aza."

Appy and Sarah both had tears at the adult Gbandi had become. Both hugged him.

Appy remarked, "You bet we love you!"

"I say yes, too!" Sadie said.

"Wow," Zenna said, "I'll have more skaters to practice with. My skating teacher will like that. I say yes!"

"More brothers," Ajani rolled his eyes. "At their age, I guess I'll have to teach them to drive. Do thirteen-year-old girls nag their brothers? Just kidding everybody, I say yes, as well."

"Oh Ajani," Appy responded, "You're getting more like your Uncle Rahl with your teasing."

"He taught me." Ajani chuckled.

"Okay kids," Appy announced. "If we're all in agreement, I'll have Iman, Paki, and Aza put on a flight for the USA."

"Wonderful, Ap," Sarah rejoiced. "We've raised some fine children. I couldn't be prouder of them."

Sammy, Jeffrey, Gus, Gerard, and Eddie were a little young to appreciate the magnitude of this meeting. They just thought they'd have more big brothers and a third sister—no biggy, the more the merrier.

Edward, now seven, hollered out, "Delightful—that's this week's spelling word, Mom."

"That's a good word, Eddie," Sarah remarked. "It fit's this occasion, nicely."

"Sure does, Son," Appy agreed.

Ajani had his own band now. He excused himself to attend an early wedding reception. In a few hours, everyone would be doing their own thing. Sarah and Appy would have some time to spend alone to talk about the new family that'd be joining them.

A couple weeks later Father Jeff picked up the three teens at the airport. He brought them back to St. Matthew until Appy and Sarah came home from work. After a while, he brought them home. He received an invite to stay for dinner. Sarah had made Ruthy's special dinner. Of course, Father Jeff couldn't wait to enjoy this meal again; even though, Sarah had made it often for him. The three teens spoke broken English, but if one listened carefully, one could understand what they were communicating. Sarah thought they were all handsome and darling teens. The once orphaned children were so excited and filled with warmth to have a mother and father again and many siblings to enjoy. Paki mentioned he was a good runner. He thought he might like track, something that Father Reed had brought up to him. Aza seemed to follow Zenna around the house. Zenna showed Aza her practice skates.

Aza said, "Maybe I do that, but cold here."

"Yes," Zenna answered. "I had a hard time getting use to the weather, but now I'm on the ice all the time. Anymore, I don't mind the cold at all."

Zenna brought the teens to their rooms and each teen was ecstatic. The three unpacked their belongings, which didn't amount to much. Later that evening, they joined the family to watch television and enjoy popcorn.

"This is good," Iman remarked.

Their new life began in a home filled with love and one that would afford them many wonderful family experiences.

CHAPTER 23

As in all families, time seemed to pass so fast. Before you know it, children are adults. Sarah knew that Appy was about to reach his fiftieth birthday. She began to make up a list of guests that she thought Appy would like with him to celebrate his birthday. There were many friends, and the clergy from St. Matthew. Moreover, her dream was to bring in Lamar, Chikae, Father Reed, and Sister Myra from Africa. It'd be her gift to her husband…. She'd pay the cost of the air flight by chartered plane. They'd also be welcome to spend a week at Appy and Sarah's home if permitted by their work schedules.

When first entering the States, a hotel reservation was set up for the first night. Father Jeff and Sister Jenny would meet with them that evening, and the next day at St. Matthew, until the party was to begin around three-o'clock at Sarah's home. Rahl would take Appy fishing on his boat so that Sarah and her girls could decorate the large great room. The caterers would also come in sometime after two-o'clock.

News came back through, Father Jeff, that Mr. Cronc was going to let Chikae come with his blessing. He asked Chikae to give Appy and family his best wishes. Lemar would take his vacation time, bring his wife, and leave the children with the grandparents. Of course, Brent thought this was a great opportunity for his son Lemar and wife to experience America. Father Reed was semi-retired, doing only weddings and funerals of late. He was delighted to accept the invitation. Sister Myra was also grateful for this joyous occasion. She thought that maybe she'd stay in the States in a home for retired nuns. Father Jeff, Sister Jenny, Father Larry, and Sister Eunice wouldn't retire until they closed the doors at St. Matthew, but maybe that would happen soon.

The night everyone came in, Sarah notified Appy she had to go shopping while he watched a baseball game. Instead, she brought foodstuff to St. Matthew for everyone. She also had a chance to talk with them, so thrilled everyone was to see each other again. Father Larry said he'd take Sarah's guests to the town mall early tomorrow in the event they needed something, but more importantly, for them to see what shopping centers are like in America. Sarah asked each to give a little speech about themselves and their friendship with Appy tomorrow night after the meal. She knew the children would be doing their own speeches. She was very surprised that Lamar could speak some English—somewhat, well, actually. He related to Sarah that he met his wife in an adult English course. She could speak English well, but wanted to write it, as well. Sarah guessed that Lamar was about forty-one years of age. He and Chikae, Sadie, and Gbandi would all be about the same age, strange enough—only nine or ten years younger than her and Appy.

Even though, everyone had aged some—the occasion of seeing each other again; going over memories; and hearing about their lives after they left Africa was just thrilling for Sarah. She knew Appy, who adored these people, would absolutely be beside himself with joy. She left St. Matthew about an hour later—letting everyone know she'd see them tomorrow at her home.

Appy and Sarah had breakfast together that next morning. When finished, Appy got his fishing gear together since Rahl was picking him up to enjoy the day on the water. Rahl had an old boat that Appy often worked on with him. "I must say," Appy, commented, "this boat is looking better and better."

"It needs a tune up, Ap. Are you game for that?" Rahl asked.

"Sure, why not, I can help you if you help me with mine." Appy answered. "However, I'd rather make it on a weekday evening before dark sets in—that way I can be home on the weekend when Sarah's not working."

After a couple of hours of fishing, Appy made mention, "It's hot out here, today. We should probably head home if we don't want to look like crisp bacon."

Rahl looked at his watch, "Oh, just a half-hour more, Ap. I thought I spotted a large bass that went under the boat just seconds ago. I'd like that for a dinner."

"Only if you invite me to participate in the feast," Appy replied.

When the boat was finally welled, Rahl drove back to his house telling Appy that he wanted to change his clothes and get the fishy smell off his hands. "In fact, Ap, I've a pair of pants and a shirt that you left in my duffle bag when we all went camping. Johnna washed them. You can change into them if you want."

"Well okay," Appy answered. "I guess I shouldn't be the only one who smells fishy around my wife, who hates the smell of fresh fish. I never realized you were such a "cleanic" Rahl."

Once they reached Appy's house, he opened the door, stepped back and said, "What's up—this place is all decorated?" He spotted a sign that said, "Happy 50th Birthday, Dad." He turned to Rahl. Rahl put his hand on Appy's shoulder as everyone came out from all the square openings in the house shouting, "Surprise, Happy 50th Birthday!"

Appy put his hand over his heart as he moved to hug Chikae, Lamar, Father Reed and Sister Myra. These were special friends that he never imagined seeing again in his lifetime. Tears fell!

"What in the world," Appy rejoiced, "I can hardly believe my eyes. I'm surely glad that Rahl had clean clothes for me, but I suppose that was planned, too."

"Sure was, Dear," Sarah said, "Everyone from Africa is spending a week with us."

"Oh, how exciting this is," Appy said gleefully as he put his arm around his wife and kissed her. It took a while, but Appy made it around to greet everyone and thank each for sharing his birthday with him. After serving and enjoying dinner, Sarah asked everyone to gather in the great room. She, then, asked if anyone would like to reminisce with, Appy.

Rahl came forward, "Well friend and brother-in-law, it seems we connected on our very first meeting. We've been through trials most people couldn't even imagine. I know you to be a considerate, genuinely kind, charitable fellow, but most importantly—my loving friend. He's so perfect, friends and family, he never even swears."

"Oh, that's so funny, Rahl." Appy chuckled.

Rahl continued, "I know today that love is a wonderful virtue because both you and Father Jeff taught me that early on in our friendship. On this your birthday, as you join me in old age, and we find ourselves in this decrepit state," he chuckled. "I want to say I love you."

"Speak for yourself, Rahl!"

The two had tears, hugged, and fist bumped.

Lamar stood up and said, "Because of you Ap, many children in a depressed country are happily enjoying their childhood in protected missions in Africa. Sisters of Amity and our French village are two communities that have just come under UN—protection. Something every one of us worked so hard to do to assure that the innocent would have a safe haven to live in."

"We've also enjoyed playing baseball with the equipment that you have sent over the years. I have you and Rahl to thank for many enjoyable days of baseball in my youth. Also good times spent with my beloved Keena who passed away many years back, but whom I still love and miss. She was a super smart dog. I need to also thank you and Rahl for the assistance in adopting, Nettie. She's a great, sis. She watches my children when my mother and father are busy. I love her, dearly. I love you, too, Ap—Happy Birthday friend!"

Appy hugged Lamar and whispered, "Lamar, you speak good English."

"Only so so," Lamar answered, "I hope to get better this week."

"No doubt you will," Appy answered.

Chikae stood up with tears surfacing. "If Lamar can get up and be so eloquent, I guess I can, too. How can I thank you enough, Ap, for what you did for me personally? My parents said, 'Be sure to just thank him repeatedly.' I was so close to being lost and young enough to wallow in self-pity. I've a good job, now. I also have attended college to advance my techniques in computer development, which I also have to credit to you. My wife and I have enjoyed the experience of being in the States. We'd like very much to live here, but Mama and Papa need us in Africa. They love their children and grandchildren. One can just imagine how it might crush them if a separation occurred again. I hope we'll be able to save enough to come to visit America again with the children someday. Mama keeps in touch with Reva's foster parents; and over the years, she and Papa have made the fifty-mile trip several times to see them. Jill and Berry always love seeing Reva. Reva always asks Jill to make her favorite cake for her."

"Wonderful," Appy nodded. "Of course," he assured Chikae, "You'll always be welcome here."

Chikae said, "I've brought back this bat that has all the names of the team players on it. It should stay with you, Coach Ap."

Strange enough; the traditional African clapping from his adopted children brought tears to Appy's eyes, Rahl's eyes, too. You might say that everyone was having some difficulty, and Sadie passed the tissue box around.

Appy couldn't help but chuckle, "Leave it to Sadie," as he grabbed a tissue while hugging her. "You're still a "little mother" to many. You're also an inspiration to womanhood, girl." Sadie now had six children of her own along with a singing career that kept Appy and Sarah busy attending concerts. She was a very accomplished woman. She also stayed her sweet self—thoroughly enjoying her dad's night.

Gbandi and Jeffrey got up to speak also. The two told humorous stories about the many trials and tribulations their father had suffered while raising twelve children.

Jeffrey raised his brows saying, "Like when Zenna, Eddie, and Paki totaled your vehicles as new and inexperienced drivers, crrunch—crrunch."

"Please, the sound of that Jeffrey makes me shiver," Appy replied.

Zenna chuckled, "I don't know about you brothers, but daddy always kissed me on the forehead and said, 'You'll do better the next time.'"

Appy frowned, "I doubt that I was that gentle with the boys. I probably said, 'You better do better the next time,' with a clenched fist."

Zenna was now thirty. Ironically, she married a pro-baseball player. She also was a professional skater and traveled a great deal for skating events and ice shows. She had three children that practically lived at their grandparent's home. Appy called her his ice princess.

Jeffrey continued, "I remember when Gbandi hit a home run right through our kitchen window. Dad said we were lucky that Mom wasn't at the window that day."

"That's for sure," Sarah responded. "I never even gave that a thought—gosh!"

Appy laughed, put his arm around Sarah, and said, "Thank goodness for dishwashers. Now you women never have to stand at the sink anymore and be in the line of fire."

Gbandi, now a father of three, took his turn, "Yeah, like the time Sammy came in your bed in the morning, Dad, without his diaper on and peed right in your eye while you laid there shouting, 'SARAH help me.' I was right at your bedroom door ready to grab Sammy to put a clean diaper on him when he sped away from me. With that said Dad, how about the time Ajani was supposed to feed Biff in the morning—forgot, leaving the bowl of dog food in the fridge." Gbandi began to laugh. "You ate it—thinking Mom had made hash that day."

"That doesn't speak well of my cooking," Sarah laughed. "He ate it all!"

By now, everyone was cracking up, but more was to come.

Sadie broke in, "I remember Dad when you told, Gus, who was only three at the time and stood staring at a tree. 'Gus, do you think that tree is going to walk away from you or something? Get in the car, son.' Gus turned around, giggled, and seriously answered, 'It can't, Dad—it only has one leg.'"

Ajani's son, who already had a cast on his leg, heard his father say, listen to this one, Son "How about the time, Dad, I jumped from

306

the picnic table to the lip of the garage overhang, missed, and fell to the concrete—breaking my wrist in four different places." He laughed, "Son can you understand, like father, like son?"

Appy added, "Ajani, we had lots of minor fractures, many nose bleeds, measles, and mumps. You name it—we experienced it. Even Mom got the seven-day measles and was sick that many days. I'll say, for the most part, we were and are lucky Mom is a pediatrician. Zenna was always good at letting her Mom know, 'Oh thank you Momma Sarah for saving my life,' every time Mom pulled a splinter out of her finger without causing her pain."

Appy continued to speak, "I also remember the time we all went out to dinner at a restaurant in our new mini bus. I forewarned the children not to order desserts because it was just too costly. We'll have dessert when we get home. When the meal was over, the server asked, 'Who wants dessert?' Gerard raised his hand thinking the server sounded a whole lot like Mom when passing out the sweets. Everyone was in shock since all the children just heard, NO DESSERT, but Gerard being just four at the time, apparently didn't understand. We all couldn't help ourselves, bursting out in laughter. The server looked at us as if to say, 'what's up,' so I said, 'that's okay, take their order for dessert.' Believe me that meal cost me a buck or two. Never let anyone kid you about things being cheaper by the dozen. I don't think so...."

Rahl commented, "That's hilarious kids. I love it!"

Ajani, clapping his hands on his knees said, "It sure is!"

All of a sudden, Father Jeff burst out laughing, "That pee in the eye really got to me, and Yuk, dog food for lunch? You're right, Rahl, that's hilarious!"

Appy stood up saying, "Okay that's enough about me. I need to say a few things about the lovely people who are here, most especially, Sister Jenny whom everyone here cherishes. She's my living guardian angel, is the soul of modesty, and has a wonderfulness about her that's hard to match. Most importantly, she radiates love when she speaks, in her deeds, and in her reverence to the Lord. I appreciate everything you have done on my behalf, Sister Jenny. For that, I love you like a mother. Your famous last words to me were, 'Appy you'll do better tomorrow.' You would then kiss me on the forehead. I know I have repeated those words to my sons and daughters. The saying, 'The fruit never falls far from the tree' has a great deal to do with the attitudes and habits of the people around us."

Zenna spoke out, "Now I know how that came about Pap Pee Daddy—oops, that just slipped out."

Appy hugged her.

"Oh, I've forgotten something," Appy continued, "I'll just add this, Sister Jenny, blushes a great deal just like my wife." He pointed to her pink cheeks, and chuckled. Appy ended by saying, "Furthermore, you're perfection little lady. No one can take that from you."

Sister Jenny raised her handkerchief, wrapped it around her index finger, and wiped the moist drops coming from the inner edges of her eyes. She walked up to Appy, placed his head between her hands, and kissed him gently on the forehead. This time he returned with the same.

"In addition," Appy announced, "I feel privileged to say a few things about, Father Jeff." He put his hand to his forehead as if deep in thought, "It's telling, Father Jeff, that the father I've always dreamed of is the spitting image of you."

Father Jeff swallowed hard, putting his fist to his mouth. Rahl walked over to Father Jeff, who was now in his seventies, and put his arm around him knowing he'd get emotional.

Appy continued, "You're humorous, and by far, the most beautiful and eloquent conversationalist that I've ever known."

Father Jeff piped in, "That's because I've listened to so many confessions," he laughed.

"See, that's what I mean," Appy chuckled. "You always know the perfect thing to say. I've always admired that in you. You're a very easy person to talk with. I also find you're a brave man who went to Africa to make a difference. Of course, I helped out with the number of children I fell in love with."

The musical clapping went on again.

"Thanks, kids, the feeling is mutual."

Appy continued, "Father, I know you to be a gentle man. One who cares about everything that exists around me, my choice in a wife, my beautiful children, even my dogs and chickens."

Father Jeff laughed again because he did enjoy feeding those chickens.

"I sense," Appy, commented, "either I was born with an innate goodness, or you and others have been of enormous importance in who I am today. Sarah and I honestly believe it is a little of both. Without you…well?"

Gbandi came close to his Dad and said, "Of course, you're right, I've often thought about that myself. I, too, came to the same conclusion. You mean so much, Dad, to so many that I think your goodness rubbed off on us."

"I hope that's true, Gbandi. This I know, Son, you certainly are a good man. You make me want to cry." Appy hugged him as tears did flow.

Father Jeff also approached Appy to embrace him.

In the large gathering room, Sarah stood next to Appy, Father Jeff, Sister Jenny, their children and grandchildren, Rahl, Johnna and their family, the Hendersons, along with all their friends from Africa, and neighbors when Father Jeff began to speak:

"My Son, all the people here are a testimony to who you are. On your fiftieth birthday, Appy, we have a present for you that will further define and complete you even more…." A silence fell over the room. Father Jeff walked over to the large French doors opening them wide. At which time, he took the hand of a beautiful mature woman, and said in a shaky voice with tears in his eyes, "Appy—this is your mother!" THE END

Sequel to "Living out a Dream" to come with "Off-color on the Lake, Book II"

AUTHOR BIOGRAPHY

At the age of fifty-seven, I received an Associate of Liberal Arts Degree and took French courses recently. My mother was French and was fluent in the language, but she never wanted her children to learn French, which I found strange. She apparently had her reasons. Ironically, the only words I learned from her were not so nice and were heard only when she was mad at someone or something. I personally think it is a beautiful language and have used a little in my story. It shouldn't distract the reader. College wasn't something my parents could hope to give their children due to circumstances that were beyond their control.

In the course of attending classes later in my life, I began to enjoy writing essay papers, even though, in the beginning my English comp. 101 teacher made mention, 'Your writings are always very mature, but all over the place. Put it together, and your works will be very good.' That was a wake up call for me. Here in "Living Out A Dream" I strived to be coherent and make this an interesting and enjoyable story for my readers.

As a wife of fifty-two years, a mother of three, a grandmother of eight, a great-grand mother of two, and at seventy-one years of age; I hope that my family will one day place my book on their coffee table in memory of my works. After all, how many grandmothers write a book. I have fallen in love with the children in "Living Out A Dream," as I am sure the reader will, as well. I also hope that the readers of "Living Out A Dream" will occasionally feel the humor in my soul. I, indeed, hope you enjoy!